4 2 2

47376

Visual Sources Series

ELIZABETHAN ENGLAND

Peter Lane

Formerly Principal Lecturer in History
Coloma College of Education, Kent

BATSFORD ACADEMIC AND EDUCATIONAL LTD London

First published 1981
© Peter Lane 1981

ISBN 0 7134 3566 6

Printed in Hong Kong
for the Publishers Batsford Academic and
Educational Ltd,
4 Fitzhardinge Street, London W1H 0AH

Acknowledgment

Figures 31 and 39 are reproduced by Gracious Permission of Her Majesty The Queen. The
Author and Publishers also thank the following for their kind permission to reproduce copy-
right illustrations: Ashmolean Museum, Oxford for fig 44; the Bodleian Library, Oxford for
figs 2, 16; The British Library for fig 35; the Trustees of the British Museum for figs 33, 42;
Country Life for figs 27, 36; the Fitzwilliam Museum, Cambridge for fig 25; the Guildhall
Art Gallery for fig 11; the Irish Tourist Board for fig 54; A.F. Kersting for figs 23, 41; the
Mansell Collection for figs 13, 19, 20, 52, 53; the National Galleries of Scotland for figs 30,
32, 51; the National Maritime Museum for figs 46, 47, 48; the National Monuments Record
for fig 38; the National Portrait Gallery, London for figs 7, 8, 9, 10, 17; The Marquess of
Salisbury for fig 18 (photograph by the Courtauld Institute); the Tate Gallery, London for
fig 4; the Marquess of Tavistock, and the Trustees of the Bedford Estates for figs 37, 50; the
Victoria and Albert Museum for figs 55, 61. Figures 28 and 49 were drawn by Mr R. Britto.
Figures 59 and 60 were drawn by Chartwell Illustrators. The other illustrations appearing in
the book are the property of the Publishers.

Contents

The Illustrations

1 The Importance of Elizabeth I's Reign and Character

An uncertain throne

Elizabeth was twenty-five years old when she came to the throne in 1558 (*pic. 1*). She was the daughter of Henry VIII and Anne Boleyn — who had been executed in 1536 when Elizabeth was only three years old. Throughout much of the rest of Henry VIII's reign she had been known as a bastard — as her father tried to persuade people that he had never been properly married to Anne Boleyn.

During the short reign of her half-brother, Edward VI, Elizabeth was the centre of Protestant plots. People did not expect Edward to live for very long and many made plans for the succession to the throne after he was dead. Few among the ruling classes wanted to see the Catholic Mary Tudor come to the throne. She was the daughter of Henry's first marriage — to the Spanish princess, Catherine of Aragon. It was feared that, if Mary became Queen,

1 A portrait of the young Elizabeth I, from an official document. Notice the orb in her left hand and the sceptre in her right hand, the jewelled bracelets and Crown and the high-necked dress. You can see other pictures of "Gloriana" in *pics. 8 and 50*.

she would try to restore Catholicism to the place it had held before Henry divorced her mother and set himself up as Supreme Head of the Church in England. The break with Rome had led to the closing of the monasteries and the grants of former monastery lands to the country gentry, lawyers, politicians, courtiers and others who were prepared to support Henry VIII against the Pope. A Catholic restoration under a Catholic Queen might lead to an attempt to bring back the monks and to rebuild the monasteries. This would mean a great loss to the men who had enriched themselves at the Church's expense. So, during Edward VI's reign Protestant nobles looked to the young Elizabeth as the centre of their Protestant hopes. The break with Rome had been caused by her father's infatuation with her mother and the Pope's refusal that Henry should divorce his first wife in order to marry her. It seemed natural that she would wish to support an anti-Catholic campaign.

During the first three years of Edward's reign, the Protector, the Duke of Somerset, ruled. His brother, Thomas Seymour, had married one of Henry VIII's former wives, Catherine Parr. When she died he tried to get himself married to Princess Elizabeth — as a means of obtaining the throne for himself. In 1549 Somerset ordered the execution of his brother on a charge of treason. The young Elizabeth learned that men's ambitions were very great and could lead to violent deaths. As we will see, she never forgot that lesson.

An uneasy Church
Throughout the reigns of Edward VI and her older sister, Queen Mary I, Elizabeth saw how religion could lead to violence. Under Edward, the Protestant Somerset pushed the Church into a more extreme Protestant position than it had occupied during Henry VIII's reign. Churches were pulled down, stained glass windows smashed, statues and altars broken and richly embroidered clothing destroyed. Catholics in Devon and Cornwall rose in rebellion — and were savagely suppressed.

And when Catholic Queen Mary I came to the throne, it was the Protestants who suffered. Edward VI's Protestant advisers were the first to be executed — for having tried to put Lady Jane Grey, the Queen's cousin, on the throne instead of Mary. Then it was the turn of Protestant bishops — Latimer and Ridley, who were burnt to death at Oxford with Latimer crying out: "Be of good comfort, Master Ridley! Play the man; we shall this day light such a candle by God's grace in England as I trust shall never be put out." Then Cranmer, the Archbishop of Canterbury under Edward VI, agreed to admit that he had been wrong to help Somerset and Northumberland, the second ruler under the boy-king Edward, make the Church more Protestant. He agreed that Catholicism was the true religion — in return for a promise that he would not be executed. But Mary's Catholic advisers betrayed him; after he had signed the various documents in which he admitted his errors, they then decided that he, too, would have to burn to death (*pic. 2*).

6

There was a Protestant rising against Mary in 1554 which ended with the execution of its leader, Sir Thomas Wyatt, and hundreds of his supporters. The Princess Elizabeth was, not unnaturally, once again the centre of Protestant hopes. Mary knew this and feared her sister. Therefore Elizabeth, who had been imprisoned in the Tower for some time, was carefully watched when she went visiting friends in one or other of the castles where Protestant nobles were biding their time (*pic. 3*). To please her sister and to win some measure of safety, Elizabeth agreed to follow the Catholic religion — while assuring her Protestant friends that she did so only out of fear.

From all this religious anarchy Elizabeth learned that the country would not be at peace until there was a religious settlement which could win the loyalty of both Catholics and Protestants. As we shall see, this was one of the main aims of her reign.

A successful reign

Elizabeth reigned from 1558 until 1603. During this long reign England achieved a large measure of religious peace, although a minority of Catholics and another minority of Puritans (extreme Protestants) continued to agitate for different changes. This religious peace was one of the reasons why England was able to enjoy a great leap forward in other directions. Elizabeth's sailors not only defeated the Spanish Armada in 1588, they also sailed in search of new trade and new lands and so helped England become economically richer while also laying the foundations of that Empire which was to be firmly established during the seventeenth century (Chapters 11 and 12).

One sign of the greater wealth were the many fine houses built for the increasing number of wealthy traders and landowners (*pic. 14*). Another sign of England's greatness under Elizabeth was the great outpouring of music, of books (*pic. 43*) and above all of great plays written by a group of playwrights of whom Shakespeare is the best known (*pic. 5*).

And the energetic, able and wise Elizabeth was largely responsible for the changed position. Late in her reign a group of MPs and Lords came to ask her to take steps to ensure that, when she died, the succession to the throne

2 The burning of Thomas Cranmer at Oxford. Notice the clothes of the onlookers for whom a burning or an execution was a chance for "a day out". Cranmer put his right hand into the flames. As he did so he cried out: "This hand hath offended". This was his attempt to make up for having signed confessions of error and an agreement that Catholicism was the true religion.

3 Kenilworth Castle, Warwickshire, as it may have appeared in 1575 when Elizabeth I stayed there. Notice the walls, moat and bridge leading to the gateway. Castles had been the centre of noblemen's power to defy even kings in the past. During the Wars of the Roses most of the old nobility had been killed off; their places at Court were taken by a new group of men and they, as well as the old nobility, turned castles from places of warfare into more comfortable homes.

would be safeguarded. In her reply she said: "Though I am a woman I have as good a courage answerable to my place as ever my father had. I am your appointed Queen. I will never be by violence constrained to do anything. I thank God I am endowed with such qualities that if I were turned out of the realm in my petticoat, I were able to live any place in Christendom." She did not tell the meeting that she had arranged for the throne to go to the King of Scotland — for that might have tempted some of them to begin the sort of plotting which had marred the reigns of Edward VI and Mary.

4 The Cholmondeley sisters and their babies. Notice the richly decorated dresses and the complicated high ruffs which stood up behind the ladies' heads. These ladies were the wives of wealthy men — and their dresses reflected their husbands' position, wealth and power. There were hundreds of such men and women — a sign of the increasing wealth of Elizabethan England.

Her character

Elizabeth did not only have her father's courage. She also had his violent temper — throwing beer into the faces of men who disagreed with her, imprisoning favourites who went too far in their claims on her friendship, and even executing Essex, whom she undoubtedly had once loved deeply (*pic. 12*).

But she had also inherited some of her mother's characteristics. Anne Boleyn had flirted with Henry VIII until she won the Crown. Unfortunately, she continued to flirt with other men after her marriage and so lost her head. Elizabeth knew how to use her womanly charm to win over the strong men by whom she was surrounded — but was wiser than her mother. She never allowed her private affections to cause her to lose sight of the fact that she was Queen while the rest were mere subjects. We shall see that her rival, Mary, Queen of Scots, did not learn that lesson and, like Anne Boleyn, suffered for her mistakes (Chapter 6).

Elizabeth was an unusual Queen because she was an unusual woman. She was highly educated and intelligent. She could speak in Greek and Latin to the professors at Oxford or Cambridge; when speaking to Italians she could speak in their language, while she also spoke fluent French to the French Ambassador (*pic. 13*). This helped to make her popular with the more educated classes. Her enemies thought of her as being sly, calling her *Inglese Italianata*. But she knew that she had to be hard and clever if she were to avoid her mother's fate, and slightly vulgar and coarse if she were to win the hearts of the sailors, courtiers and politicians on whom she relied. So she learned how to use her beauty, her jewels and clothes (*pics 1, 8 and 18*) as weapons with which to win men's admiration and help.

A shrewd Queen

She was indeed a Queen who worked out carefully exactly what she wanted and how she might get it. Her religious settlement was a good example of this calculating policy. Under Edward VI, the extreme Protestants had tried to force their ideas on people — and there had been uprisings. Mary had tried to push her total Catholicism on an unwilling people — and again there had been uprisings. Elizabeth's settlement did not try to push any extremist ideas;

5 Shakespeare's birthplace. Notice the timber framework of the house, the bay windows on the first floor and the smaller windows on the second floor. Notice too the way in which the windows were of small panes of glass held in place with strips of lead. The wealthy could afford more splendid houses than this, which is typical of the homes of the increasing number of town merchants, successful traders and industrialists.

it was a *via media*, a halfway house in which, she hoped, both extremes could find a home.

She was equally calculating when it came to the question of marriage. She allowed some of her favourites to think that they might win her hand — Leicester (*pic. 9*), Raleigh (*pic. 10*), Essex all had their high hopes. She also allowed the French Duke of Anjou to hope that he might become her husband, while also toying for a while with the suggestion of Philip II, King of Spain (*pic. 7*), that, having married Mary Tudor, he might now marry the Queen Elizabeth. But she never allowed her heart to overrule her head; nor did she allow Leicester or Essex to take the place of the shrewd but unglamorous Cecil as her most important Minister (*pic. 16*).

She was equally careful and shrewd when it came to the question of making war. Some of her hot-headed supporters wanted to make war on Spain or to help the Protestant cause in war-torn Europe. But Elizabeth knew that she was really a poor Queen. Even during wartime her income was never more than £500,000 and in peacetime her Parliaments would not agree to increases in taxation. This meant that she never had the money to pay for a large army or to support a massive navy. She never even had enough money to reward those who fought for her — she had to allow them to enrich themselves out of booty taken from Spanish treasure ships or from privileges in trade and industry. This again helps to explain why she was careful to use her womanly charm to win the support of those on whom she relied to give their time and sometimes their lives in her battles. And it also explains why she was careful to follow the policy which she outlined in a poem:

Queen

Queen Eliz: visiting her Camp at Tilbury being mounted on Horseback with a Truncheon of an ordinary Captain in her hand

6 One of the cards in a pack made in 1588. This one showed Elizabeth visiting her troops and fleet at Tilbury, where they were preparing to meet the Armada. Her courage and coarseness appealed to her fighting-men, to whom she appeared as the Queen of Hearts in this pack.

The Daughter of Debate,
whom discord eke doth sow,
Shall reap no gain where former rule
hath taught still peace to grow.

Mary, Queen of Scots, "The Daughter of Debate", lost her throne and her life. Elizabeth "taught still peace to grow", so that men grew prosperous in peaceful England while the rest of Europe was ablaze with religious wars.

Long to reign over us
For forty-five years Elizabeth was both Queen and Prime Minister. "A mere woman", she led the country in times of peace and war (*pic. 6*), although she was never physically very strong — suffering from those Tudor tantrums which took their toll of her nerves. And during her reign England emerged as one of the leading nations of Europe, firmly set on the path which was to enable her to overcome Spain, Holland and France, and to become in the eighteenth century the world's first industrial power.

THE YOUNG HISTORIAN

1 Look at *pic. 1* and write the headlines which might have appeared above reports of (i) Queen Mary's death and (ii) Elizabeth I's accession, in newspapers owned by (a) Catholics, (b) Protestants and (c) a Spaniard.
2 Look at *pic. 2* and write the account which might have appeared about this burning in newspapers owned by (a) Catholics and (b) Protestants.
3 Draw or paint your own "Rich women and their children", using *pic. 4* as a model.
4 Look at *pic. 5* and write the account which might have appeared in a local newspaper in Stratford of the success of William Shakespeare in London.
5 In *pic. 5* you can see the leaded windows which made Elizabethan homes less draughty and much lighter than previous houses had been. Using strips of tape and transparent paper you can make your own leaded window — and you might put in a coloured coat of arms as shown in *pic. 42*.
6 Look at *pic. 6* and write the newspaper account which might have described this visit. (The reporter might have mentioned the Queen's clothing and that of her courtiers, her ability to ride, the cheering of the crowds, the anger at Spanish plans to invade England and at Catholic plots to overthrow the popular Queen.)
7 Write the newspaper account which might have been produced after an interview between one of Elizabeth's followers and a commentator who tried to find out what her followers thought about the Queen, her temper, her marriage plans, her religious beliefs and her character in general.

11

2 Elizabeth, Her Favourites and Marriage Prospects

The importance of the marriage question

One of the most important problems facing Queen Elizabeth was the possibility of her marriage. Should she marry the Spanish King (*pic. 7*) or one of his relations? Should she marry a French Prince? Or should she choose a husband from the ranks of the English nobility?

English politicians like Cecil (*pic. 16*) and Walsingham (*pic. 17*) were concerned about her marriage plans — because they were anxious about the succession to the English throne. If Elizabeth did not marry, or if, having married, she left no children, then the best claim to the throne would rest with the young Mary Stuart, Queen of Scots (*pic. 29*). But Mary Stuart was a Catholic and she might try to lead the sort of Catholic revival that had caused

7   Philip II of Spain, the husband of Queen Mary I. He saw himself as the Catholic champion in Europe as well as the ruler of Spain and its Empire. He was hated by English Protestants and by English traders and merchants. After the defeat of the Armada in 1588 he was less of a threat.

so much trouble during the reign of Queen Mary. Mary Stuart was also married to the heir to the throne and later King of France, and if she became Queen of England, this would make for a strong French-English alliance in Europe.

Philip of Spain

Philip of Spain had been married to the Catholic Queen Mary (*pic. 26*). He had supported his wife's attempts to win England back to Catholicism. Now that Elizabeth was Queen, Philip wanted that attempt to continue; he thought of himself as the leader of the Catholic revival throughout Europe. So he proposed marriage to Elizabeth almost as soon as Mary was dead.

By such a marriage Philip would also have prevented a strong English-French alliance. On the contrary he would have created a strong English-Spanish power-bloc, and would have been the better able to put down French attempts to win more power in Europe.

This rivalry between Spain and France was of great benefit to Elizabeth. For as long as the Queen did not marry, both sides could hope that she would, in the end, choose a husband from their country. And while both sides had that hope, neither would be anxious to make war against England for fear of driving Elizabeth into an alliance with the other side.

Why not a Spaniard?

Elizabeth kept Philip waiting for an answer to his marriage proposal. She knew that if she married Philip, she would have to become a Catholic — and she also knew that this would lead to unrest in England. She also knew that the majority of Englishmen, Catholic as well as Protestant, hated Spain which claimed to rule the largest part of the world and tried to stop English traders from expanding their business in Asia, Africa and America.

Once she was sure that she was firmly on the throne, Elizabeth told Philip that she would not marry him. But she did agree to listen to the marriage proposal of one of his cousins, the Archduke, Charles of Austria. Philip decided to make the best of a bad job; if he could not have Elizabeth for himself, better that she married one of his relatives than that she married a Frenchman. And so, for eight years, ambassadors came from the Archduke pleading his cause and asking for an answer — and for eight years Elizabeth continued to agree to listen to these appeals but to give no definite answer.

At the same time she received well-publicized proposals of marriage from members of the royal houses of Scotland, Sweden and France. And while there were so many Princes anxious to win her hand — and a claim on England's power — there was no chance that either France or Spain would attack England. This gave Elizabeth the time she needed to sort out the religious problem (Chapter 4), to secure the peace which industry and trade needed if England was to grow richer, and to win the support of the mass of the people, for whom life improved as a result of the long peace.

The Duke of Anjou

Mary, Queen of Scots, had married the heir to the French throne. In 1559 he became King of France, so that Mary became Queen of France as well as of Scotland. Unfortunately for her, her husband died in 1560, leaving her free, as we shall see, to return to her native Scotland (Chapter 6).

Two brothers of the dead King followed him in turn on the French throne, and the youngest brother, Hercules, who became Duke of Anjou, was next in line. Elizabeth allowed him to propose marriage to her and kept him waiting for an answer. Indeed, as late as 1579-80 Elizabeth accepted his presents, the pleas of his ambassadors, and even two visits from the Prince himself, whom she described as "my frog". But Elizabeth was never seriously interested in tying her throne to that of Catholic France. She only used this unfortunate Prince as a pawn in the game she was playing in Europe. In 1579 Philip of Spain was trying to put down the rebellion against him in the Netherlands (modern Belgium and Holland), sending troops to help the anti-English rebels in Ireland, and threatening war against the English sea-dogs who were attacking his Empire in Central and South America. Elizabeth did not want to go to war against Spain. She let it become known that she was thinking of marrying the Duke of Anjou — in the hope that this would cool Philip's temper and make it less likely that he would make war against England. And once that danger died down, so Elizabeth's interest in the Duke declined.

◄ 8   Queen Elizabeth standing on Saxton's map of England in 1592. Her feet were on Ditchley in Oxfordshire where she stayed as the guest of Sir Henry Lee, whose cousin, Captain Thomas Lee, was executed in 1601 for trying to rescue Essex from the Tower. The artist was careful not to show the Queen as she really was — a sixty-year-old woman, worn out by the burdens of power. On the right you can see the lines of a poem which began: "The Prince of Light, the Sun by whom things live. Of heaven the glory, and of earth the grace." Flattery was one way to the favour of a fading beauty.

9   Robert Dudley, Earl of Leicester, as he was when he became Elizabeth's favourite. When his stepson, Essex, became the Queen's favourite, Leicester was an old man, his beard white. But he hoped, even then, to win back the Queen's affection through the influence of his proud stepson.

Robert Dudley, Earl of Leicester

If Elizabeth was unwilling to take a husband from the ranks of foreign princes, maybe she would choose one from among the English nobility. This is what some of her favourites thought and hoped. But they did not understand the cautious, complex and ruthless Elizabeth. For she realized that, if she chose one of the nobility for her husband, this would anger other noblemen who might be tempted to plot with Mary, Queen of Scots, or some other claimant to the throne. If she chose a Catholic nobleman, what would the Protestant majority do? If she chose an extremist Protestant as a husband, what would the Catholic nobles and the less extreme Protestants do? And would a forceful husband lead her into war with Spain when she wanted peace?

So, as we know, Elizabeth did not choose an English husband. But for many years Robert Dudley, the son of the Duke of Northumberland who was executed by the Queen Mary, seemed to be her chosen favourite. Certainly she was fond of the handsome and ambitious Dudley, who later became the Earl of Leicester (*pic. 9*). And he was as ambitious as his father had been. Certainly Cecil and others of Elizabeth's more cautious Ministers feared that she might agree to marry him — even though he was already married, but living apart from his neglected and unhappy wife, the former Amy Robsart.

At a time when rumours of a marriage between Dudley and Elizabeth were commonplace, there came the news that, conveniently for Dudley, his wife

10 Sir Walter Raleigh, as seen by an artist in 1588, the year of the Armada. Notice the embroidered clothing and fine cloak. The well-to-do lived well in Elizabeth's time.

had died by falling down the stairs in her home. Although the verdict of an inquest was that she had died "accidentally", there were plenty of people willing to agree that Dudley had played some part in her death. Elizabeth was wise enough to see that to marry the widowed Dudley would offend too many of her subjects. So, although she continued to show him affection and may have taken him as a lover, she did not choose him as a possible husband.

Sir Walter Raleigh

There were other courtiers who thought that they had a chance to win Elizabeth's hand. Perhaps the best known of these was Sir Walter Raleigh (*pic. 10*). He was a half-brother to Sir Humphrey Gilbert, MP for Plymouth and one of the leading seamen of the time. Like Gilbert and Drake and other West Countrymen, Raleigh was a sailor who had fought against Spain and a dashing soldier who had taken part in land battles against the Spanish. He was tall, handsome, popular and very intelligent — being a good poet and the author of a *History of the World*. It is not surprising that this "all-round" man gained Elizabeth's favour. She gave him a large grant of land in Ireland and the right to set up English settlements in North America — to which he gave the name Virginia, in honour of the unmarried Queen.

But the arrogance of the proud Raleigh offended too many of Elizabeth's more cautious Ministers, and she had the sense to see that while she might be flattered by Raleigh and might amuse herself with him for idle moments, she could not afford to take him for a husband.

The Earl of Essex

Robert Devereux, the son of the First Earl of Essex, succeeded to the title in 1576, when his father died and when he was only nine years old. His mother then married the Earl of Leicester (*pic. 9*) who regarded his stepson as a protégé whose career he should encourage. Before long the brilliant Earl of Essex had outshone his aging stepfather, once the Queen's favourite, and had himself become the favourite of a now aging Queen. He led military and naval expeditions on her behalf in the Netherlands and elsewhere. He had become himself the patron of other eminent men, such as the writers Francis Bacon and Shakespeare. He became the leader of a group of ambitious, able and intelligent courtiers which included Raleigh and Shakespeare's patron, the Earl of Southampton.

In 1596 Essex was commander-in-chief of the land forces which raided Cadiz, where Philip was planning a second Armada against England. Essex's forces stormed and sacked the town and two other nearby ports. The damage was so great that Philip was driven into bankruptcy; he had to announce that he could not pay his debts and so ruined many of his people who had sold him materials and supplies.

The success of this and other attacks and the evident weakness of Spain

17

11 A view of part of the Thames below London Bridge. Notice on the South Bank the Globe Theatre and the bear-baiting centre, and along the North Bank the many fine houses of the nobility — Somerset, Arundel, Essex. The river was London's main thoroughfare and a trip by boat was quicker, safer and more pleasant than walking through the streets.

inspired Essex and his warlike companions to ask that Elizabeth continue to make war on Spain even after Philip had died in 1598. Cecil, Elizabeth's long-serving and cautious Minister, had died just before Philip, and Essex and his friends had their way.

At the same time Ireland rose in rebellion (Chapter 10). Essex asked to be appointed Lord Lieutenant of Ireland (*pic. 55*). But he found that fighting a guerilla war in the wilds of Ireland was different from fighting pitched battles against the Spaniards. Within a year his forces had been weakened in a series of small battles and Essex decided to make a truce with the rebels. This angered Elizabeth. So her favourite sailed back to England, confident that he would be able to win the Queen's support for his policy.

He was still covered in mud from having ridden to London when he burst into the Queen's room where she was discussing affairs with her new chief

Minister, Robert Cecil. The Queen was annoyed at Essex's arrogance at having forced his way into her royal presence. She listened to the advice of Cecil and arrested Essex. He was kept in house custody for several months, deprived of his many positions of command and of the royal grant which was his main income.

Overproud Essex

For ten or so years Elizabeth had flirted with the dashing young courtier who had persuaded himself that he was too important for the aging Queen to ignore. He did not realize that the wise old Queen had allowed Leicester and others to pay court to her — but had followed her own policies and those of Cecil. She had allowed the dashing young Essex to flatter her with his poems and songs — but kept William Cecil and now his son Robert as her closest advisers. Essex thought that he had the power and popularity to rid the Queen of her more cautious advisers and so gain power — and perhaps the Queen's hand in marriage for himself.

So, at his home on the River Thames (*pic. 11*), he and his followers plotted the overthrow of Robert Cecil and the Council. On 7 February 1601 Essex and his friends paid Southampton's company of actors to put on Shakespeare's *Richard II*. In this play Shakespeare showed how a rebel, Henry Bolingbroke,

12   The death warrant of the Earl of Essex. Notice Elizabeth's firm signature on top of the document, which was addressed to Thomas Agerton, the Lord Keeper of the Tower. Southampton and other plotters were to be hung, drawn and quartered. But, the document went on, Essex was not to suffer these indignities. Elizabeth declared that it was "our pleasure . . . to have the head of the said Robert, Earl of Essex, cut off at the Green within our Tower of London".

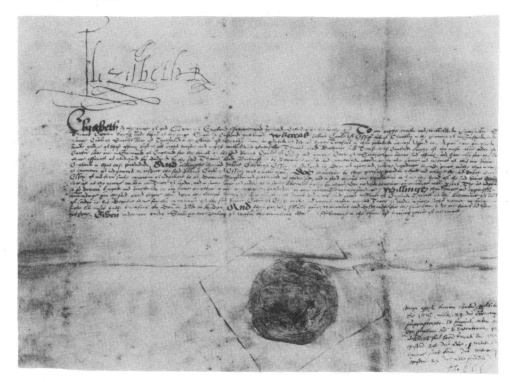

had overthrown a ruling but unpopular King. After seeing the play, Essex and his friends went back to Essex House. The Council suspected that Essex had asked for this particular play as part of his campaign to whip up support for his projected attack on Elizabeth (now unpopular and aging). Messengers were sent to ask Essex to appear before the Council to explain his choice of play.

Essex refused to go to see the Council. Instead, he gathered a band of swordsmen-friends, rode into the City along the Strand, and tried to stir up popular support with a cry that there was a plot against his life by the Queen's "false counsellors". But none of the Londoners followed him — much to his surprise. And when he tried to ride back home he found that the Queen's supporters had blocked his way at Ludgate. He had to slip down to the River Thames and make his way home by boat.

Here he was arrested, taken to the Tower, and a few days later executed along with five of his main supporters (*pic. 12*). This was a sad ending to the last love story of Queen Elizabeth who herself was to die two years later, making way for James VI of Scotland whose son Charles was himself to die on another scaffold.

THE YOUNG HISTORIAN

1 Write the headlines which might have appeared above reports of Philip's proposal of marriage to Elizabeth I, in newspapers owned by (i) Spaniards, (ii) Frenchmen, (iii) English Catholics, (iv) English Protestants.
2 Write the letter which might have been sent by one of Elizabeth's Ministers explaining why she would not marry either Philip of Spain or the Duke of Anjou.
3 Write the letter which one of the courtiers might have written complaining of the Queen's affection for *either* Leicester (*pic. 9*) *or* Essex.
4 Write the account of the death of Leicester's wife as it might have appeared in newspapers (i) favourable, and (ii) opposed to Leicester.
5 Write the account of Essex's ride through London in 1601 as it might have been given by an eye-witness.
6 Paint or draw "Our Glorious Queen" (*pic. 8*).
7 Make a poster which might have been used by Essex and Southampton to advertize the production of *Richard II*.
8 Write the letter which you might have sent after a journey by boat along the Thames (*pic. 11*). (You might have written about the great houses with steps leading down to the river, the ships carrying goods to and from England, the Tower with its Traitor's Gate — *pic. 20*.)
9 Write the headlines which might have appeared above reports of Essex's death, in newspapers which (i) supported, and (ii) opposed him.

3 Elizabeth's Ministers

The Queen rules

Today the government's policies are those of whichever political party has a majority in the House of Commons. The most important political person in our country is the Prime Minister. It was not like that in Elizabeth I's time. She was not only the Queen; she was also the head of her government — and her own Prime Minister. Ambassadors from Spain, France and other countries came to find out what her policies were and to tell her what their royal masters would like her to do (*pic. 13*).

Courtiers and servants

But not even the energetic and able Elizabeth could handle alone all the work involved in governing the country. She had to choose men to help her. Previous Kings and Queens had had to do this also. You may have heard about Henry VIII's leading minister, Thomas, Cardinal Wolsey. He was the son of an Ipswich

13 Elizabeth I receives a foreign ambassador. One of the main reasons why Kings and Queens sent ambassadors to foreign countries was to learn as much as they could about the policies of other Kings and Queens. Ambassadors made friends with as many people as possible, tried to find out who were opposed to the monarch and who might take part in plots against him or her.

butcher; but he had been able to go to University, became a priest, received an appointment in the household of the then Archbishop of Canterbury, and in time won himself the favour of Henry VII and Henry VIII. While serving his King, Wolsey had the chance to serve himself. He became a very rich man, able to pay for the building of the magnificent palace of Hampton Court as his main home.

Here we have one reason why men were willing — and indeed anxious — to serve their monarch. Such service brought great opportunities for becoming very wealthy. A grateful monarch might give large areas of land to a favourite Minister — and in that way men like Raleigh could become rich. There were various government jobs for which there were large salaries to be earned — and a Minister had the chance of getting one or more of these jobs. There were many examples of men who gained advancement through royal service. Sir Nicholas Bacon was the son of the man who had supervised the work of the shepherds at the monastery of Bury St Edmunds. Like Wolsey, he went to University, after which he became a lawyer. In 1537 he became a member of the Court of Augmentations and in 1546 a member of the Court of Wards at a salary of £90 a year. In 1558 he became Lord Keeper at a salary of £1,200 a year. By the end of his life his annual income from government positions was £5,500 a year. He owned 30 villages, where the tenant farmers paid him rents. He also owned three large country houses. His son, Francis Bacon, was to become Lord Chancellor under James I.

Great houses and religion

Henry VIII and his then chief Minister, Thomas Cromwell, had seized all the lands once owned by the monasteries. They had sold these to the people who had money to buy them. In this way new families became owners of large estates. An old rhyme says that: "Wyndham, Popham, Horner and Thynne, when the monks went out they went in", and you probably know the rhyme about "Little Jack Horner" who bought "a plum" of an estate. Sir John Thynne had served the Duke of Somerset during the reign of Edward VI. Somerset was executed in 1552, and Thynne had to spend two years as a prisoner in the Tower of London. When he was released he returned to his Wiltshire estate and set about building his great house of Longleat (*pic. 14*). Even the outside of the house gives an impression of great wealth — as did the great homes built by other rising and powerful men of this period.

And inside, these great houses provided their owners with a comfort which had never been enjoyed by the older nobility in their draughty and sparsely furnished castles. In *pic. 15* you can see the King's bedchamber at Knole, a great house near Sevenoaks in Kent. This house had once belonged to Thomas Cranmer. Henry VIII took it from him in 1538 and Queen Elizabeth gave it to her cousin, Thomas Sackville, the first Earl of Dorset. The furniture, open

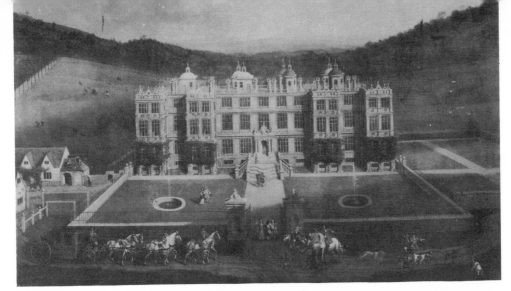

14 Longleat, one of the first great Elizabethan country-houses, built by Sir John Thynne in the 1570s.

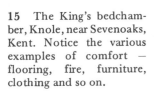

fires, carpeting and leaded windows were, like the clothes worn by their wives, an outward sign of the wealth of the new landowners.

The Cecils

Elizabeth had a large number of advisers and Ministers. But there were three men who, more than any others, were her leading Ministers. When she first came to the throne she chose William Cecil as her chief Minister (*pic. 16*). He was born in 1520, the eldest son of a rich squire of Burghley, Northants. Like Wolsey and Bacon, he had gone to University, got a job at Court, and in 1548 became private secretary to Somerset. In 1549 Somerset's opponents sent Cecil to the Tower of London, but he was released in January 1550 on taking an oath of loyalty to the new government. He was so able that he won his way back to favour, and in 1551 he became Sir William Cecil. During Mary I's reign he became a Catholic in order to save his royal job, but as

15 The King's bedchamber, Knole, near Sevenoaks, Kent. Notice the various examples of comfort — flooring, fire, furniture, clothing and so on.

16 William Cecil, the first Lord Burghley. Although his clothing was warm and comfortable, it was not as "dashing" or expensive as that of the majority of the Queen's courtiers (*pics. 9 and 10*). Notice the coat of arms on the left of the picture; Cecil paid a herald to prove that his ancestry could be traced back to Owen Whyte who "came with Harold that was Earl Godwin's son out of Cornwall". The new landowners of Elizabethan England were anxious to prove that they came from ancient families — like the old nobility.

soon as Mary became ill, Cecil went out of his way to make friends with Elizabeth who made him her chief Minister as soon as she came to the throne. He became Lord High Treasurer in 1572, the year after he had been given the title of Lord Burghley.

For forty years of Elizabeth's reign, Cecil, or Burghley, was the man on whose advice Elizabeth most relied — even if she did not always follow it. Cecil, like his Queen, was anxious to avoid a return to the religious anarchy of the last two reigns. The religious settlement (Chapter 4) was as much his as hers. Like his Queen, Cecil was also anxious to build up the nation's industry and trade, and this aim led him (and the Queen) to want to avoid war. He saw the danger of the Catholic revival in Europe, and it was Cecil's policy to weaken Spanish influence in the Netherlands and French influence in Scotland.

If Cecil served his Queen and country well, he also served the interests of his own family. Nicholas Bacon (see page 22) could build Gorhambury Hall and see to it that his son, Francis, would become even more important than he had been himself. William Cecil was more powerful than Nicholas Bacon, and so it is not surprising that he should have made his family even richer than the Bacons. In 1596 he persuaded the Queen to appoint his son, Robert, as her chief Minister. Robert succeeded to the title of Lord Burghley on William's death in 1598. A delicate man, he had to put up with the sneers of the ambitious men who surrounded Essex, and knew that even the Queen laughed at her "crook-backed dwarf". But Robert Cecil had great influence with the Queen. It was he who got Essex tried and condemned for treason, and he who saw to it that on Elizabeth's death the throne went, smoothly, to James Stuart of Scotland. James rewarded him by making him the first Earl of Salisbury, although he forced him to give up his fine home at Theobalds in exchange for the royal palace at Hatfield, where Robert built a fine new home, fitting for the leading family in the land.

Francis Walsingham *(pic. 17)*

Leicester *(pic. 9)*, Raleigh *(pic. 10)*, Essex, Dorset, and Drake *(pic. 48)* were typical of the dashing courtiers who fawned on the great Queen. But the more

17   Sir Francis Walsingham, Elizabeth's great spy-
master.

soberly dressed Cecils (*pic. 16*) and Francis Walsingham had much more influence on the policies that she followed.

Walsingham was born in Chislehurst in Kent in 1530. He went to University where, like many of his fellow students, he became a Protestant. While Queen Mary reigned, Walsingham toured Europe. When Elizabeth succeeded to the throne he returned to England and offered his services to William Cecil. Cecil sent Walsingham back to Europe with instructions that he was to send back reports of anything that might be of interest to the Queen and her Ministers. In 1569 Cecil called him back and told him to set up the country's first secret service organization. But before he could do this properly, the Queen and

Cecil sent him to France as Ambassador with orders to find out what the French intended to do about Scotland and the Netherlands. Walsingham stayed in France until 1573, spending his own small fortune on maintaining an embassy and paying a small army of spies and informers.

In 1573 he returned to England to be appointed Minister in charge of foreign policy. He was aware of the danger of Spanish or French plots to get rid of Elizabeth, so that a Catholic might succeed to the throne. And so, while looking after foreign affairs, Walsingham also built up a large spy ring inside England. This provided him with warnings of plots against the Queen. In 1577 he was given the title of Sir Francis Walsingham by the grateful Elizabeth.

Walsingham's spies brought warning of the preparations of the Spanish Armada to attack. Using their information, Walsingham was able to advise the Queen that attacks on Spanish ports would put off the date of the projected invasion. And while Drake and Essex were the ones who earned the public cheers for the raids on Cadiz and other ports, they owed much of their success, in fact, to the quiet work of Walsingham's secret service.

It was Walsingham's spies in Europe and in England itself who supplied the information that led to the trial and execution of Mary, Queen of Scots (Chapter 6). When the Jesuits and other Catholic priests came to try to help

◄ **18** This portrait of Elizabeth I is in Hatfield House, the home of the Cecil family. It is known as the "Ermine" portrait, from the little animal on her arm. Notice the lace ruff around her neck, the jewels on the fine gown and the way in which the artist, Hilliard, caught the hard features of this cautious Queen.

19 The torturing of Protestants in prison inside Lollard's Tower.

English Catholics, it was Walsingham's men who tracked them down. Many of these priests were tortured to give information which Walsingham could use against them at a later trial.

Walsingham, like other courtier-politicians, made a great deal of money from serving his Queen. He was given a number of official positions, including that of the Chancellor of the Duchy of Lancaster. But he spent most of his income on payments to spies and informers.

He was a fervent Protestant who thought that Catholics and other opponents of his Queen deserved to be tortured and imprisoned in the Tower before being executed. Walsingham died in 1590 a poor man — unlike the more cautious and businesslike Burghley.

THE YOUNG HISTORIAN

1 Write the letter which might have been sent by either the French or the Spanish Ambassador (*pic. 13*) about (i) the influence of William Cecil (*pic. 16*), (ii) the work of Sir Francis Walsingham (*pic. 17*).

2 Write the letter which might have been sent by one of the old nobility (*pic. 13*) on the rise of new families with their large incomes and homes (*pic. 14*). (He might have complained of the way they got jobs, the size of their incomes, their influence over the Queen, their University education, etc.)

3 Write the letter which might have been sent by someone who was a servant at Knole (*pic. 15*). (He or she might have written about the size of the house, the furniture, the windows, paintings, flooring, clothing and the great fires which needed huge chimneys.)

4 Write an account which might have appeared in a local newspaper when Longleat (*pic. 14*) or some other great house (i) was being built, (ii) was opened to the public for the first time after its completion.

5 Write the letter which might have been sent by someone who had seen a torturing. (Why was the person being tortured? What did Walsingham hope to learn? What sorts of torture were used? What happened to the tortured person after he had confessed?)

6 Write the headlines which might have appeared above reports of: (i) the visit of the Queen to one of the great houses, (ii) the arrest of William Cecil in 1549, (iii) the appointment of Robert Cecil in 1598, (iv) the death of the first Lord Burghley.

7 Make up the obituaries (or death notices) which might have appeared on the deaths of Nicholas Bacon, Lord Burghley, Sir Francis Walsingham.

8 Paint or draw your own version of (i) a great house (*pic. 14*), and (ii) Our Great Queen (*pic. 18*).

4 The Religious Settlement

Henry VIII's revolution

Martin Luther and other Protestant leaders had led a movement against the Roman Catholic Church in Germany, Switzerland and France from about 1520. Henry VIII had written a book condemning Luther's ideas. In return the Pope had given this fervently Catholic King the title *Fidei Defensor*, or Defender of the Faith. You can still see the letters F.D. on modern British coins.

But in the 1530s Henry wanted to divorce Queen Catherine of Aragon so that he might be free to marry Anne Boleyn. The Pope refused to agree to such a divorce, and in a series of Acts of Parliament Henry created a Church of England of which he was Supreme Head. A few people opposed him — Thomas More, for example, who was executed. A few monks also opposed him — and Henry's chief Minister, Thomas Cromwell, seized all the lands and property belonging to all the monks and nuns in England and Wales.

Most of this land was sold to the rich men who wanted land on which to build new homes. The Sidneys built much of Penshurst; Thomas Wriothesley

20   The Traitor's Gate of the Tower of London on the River Thames. The river came right up to the walls of the Tower, so that prisoners were brought by boat to, and through, this Gate.

built Beaulieu — and got the title of the Earl of Southampton; Thynne built Longleat (*pic. 14*); the Cecils built Theobalds and, later, Hatfield — all out of the spoils of the monastic lands.

There was only one major protest about this destruction of the monasteries for the enrichment of "the new men". Robert Aske led Yorkshiremen on a Pilgrimage of Grace in 1536. But the King persuaded Aske to disband his rebellious army — after which he seized Aske and had him executed in York.

Religious anarchy

Henry VIII claimed that he had not founded a new Church; he thought that he was still a good Catholic — although no longer obedient to the Pope. And even after his break with Rome he continued to punish anti-Catholic preachers, although towards the end of his life he was veering more towards Protestantism. After his death the Protestants gained more influence during the short reign of the young Edward VI, who died when he was only sixteen. Many Catholics were arrested, tried and imprisoned by the Protector, Somerset.

When the Catholic Queen Mary came to the throne she did the same to the Protestants (*pic. 2*). We have seen that the cautious William Cecil saved himself and his wealth by becoming a Catholic during this reign. So did many others, including the Vicar of Bray. He was a Church of England Catholic under Henry VIII, a Protestant under Edward VI, a Catholic again under Queen Mary and a Protestant under Elizabeth I. He claimed that "he had seen some martyrs burnt at Windsor and found the fire too hot for his tender temper".

21 A public beheading with the long sword.

22 Elizabeth I at the ► opening of one of her Parliaments.

He was accused of being a traitor or a turncoat. "Not so", he argued, "for I always keep my principle, which is this — to live and die the Vicar of Bray". And he did.

Elizabeth's hopes
During the reign of her half-sister, Queen Mary, Princess Elizabeth had followed the Catholic religion. Like Cecil and the Vicar of Bray, she wanted to live. When she came to the throne she knew that she had to try to find some way of settling the religious problem. She did not want to see the burnings (*pic. 2*) and the executions (*pic. 21*) which had been commonplace during the last two reigns. Nor did she want her people to waste their time and energy on quarrelling over religion; she wanted them to concentrate on other things — trade, industry, the Spanish and French threats to England, and the building of an overseas Empire.

The great debate, 1558-59
During the early months of her reign, it was apparent that Elizabeth would have liked to go back to the religious practices of her father, Henry VIII. But the Parliament (*pic. 22*) which met in January 1559 showed that this was not possible. The majority of the men in the House of Commons demanded that Elizabeth should insist on the use of the second (and Protestant) prayer book which had been produced during the reign of Edward VI. On the other hand, some members of the House of Lords wanted to hold on to the Catholic

practices which had been used during Queen Mary's reign. The bishops and the clergy also generally opposed the more Protestant views of the Commons.

The Elizabethan Settlement

The two Houses of Parliament debated the religious question for three months before a settlement was reached. The settlement that was eventually reached was notable for three things. In the first place, it disappointed the more extreme Protestants and the House of Commons. Secondly, it displeased the Catholic-minded bishops and clergy because it did not re-establish the Catholic religion. But perhaps the most important thing about this settlement was that it was a State settlement of the religious question; the Queen wanted it, her Ministers wanted it, and while the bishops and clergy didn't on the whole want it, they had to put up with the new religion.

Elizabeth tried to pacify the Catholics by claiming that she was only "Supreme Governor" and not, as her father had claimed, "Supreme Head of the Church of England". She appointed Commissioners, with instructions to seek out religious heretics — heresy being defined as anything condemned in Scripture or by the decisions of the first four Councils of the Church (which had met between 325 and 451). Elizabeth hoped that this would mean the end of the burnings and executions of people who opposed some more recent religious decisions.

The Act of Uniformity compelled people to attend services in their parish church. Here the Edwardian Protestant prayer book must be used — but Elizabeth insisted on important changes to its wording. There was to be no reference to "the detestable enormities" of the Roman Catholic church; people had to kneel when receiving Communion — which meant that part of the Edwardian book had to be cut, because it had explained why people ought to stand at the altar rails; there was an important alteration in the words of that second Edwardian prayer book when Elizabeth insisted that some words from the first book should be put in, that Christ was really and truly present in the Sacrament. The Act also laid down that priests and other ministers must use the copes, albs and other vestments which had been used when Edward VI came to the throne.

All this was a sincere attempt to placate the Catholics. They were also pleased by later decisions such as that the clergy were not to marry — without the permission of their bishop and a local magistrate. But the Catholics were not satisfied; they wanted a return to obedience to Rome. However, Elizabeth knew that there were too many people opposed to such a return which might have meant the loss of their lands. It was not only the Cecils, Thynnes, Walsinghams and others who had gained from the distribution of Church land. There were thousands of prosperous farmers and traders who had built comfortable homes on land which had been owned by monks or nuns. They were the people for whom the Protestant Commons spoke —

32

23 Brewer Street Farm, Bletchingley, the sort of home where prosperous Elizabethans lived.

and Elizabeth could not ignore their opinion. She needed their support if she were to hold on to her throne and oppose Spanish and French ambitions.

Establishing the Settlement
All of the bishops, except one, were dismissed from their positions for having opposed the Settlement. Sixteen heads of colleges at Oxford and Cambridge were sacked. Clergy had to sign a declaration that the prayer book was in agreement with the Word of God.

24 The signature of Elizabeth I taken from a letter written to the Earl of Lennox in 1570.

With new bishops in charge of her Church, Elizabeth persuaded the Church Assembly — or Convocation — to publish the Thirty Nine Articles which clergy and people had to obey.

Nevertheless, it was one thing for the Queen, Parliament and Convocation to lay down the law. It was another thing to get those laws obeyed. It was the local magistrates in their manor houses who had to see that the laws were put into practice — and in many parts of the country these magistrates were Catholics. In the North of England there were noblemen who would not allow the Queen's Commissioners to inspect the parishes on their estates. In Hereford the people welcomed ministers who were turned out of their livings because they refused to accept the Settlement.

In the next three chapters we shall see how the Catholics and the extremist Protestants reacted to the moderate Settlement by which Elizabeth hoped to win the support of the whole country. She saw her Church as a *via media,* a middle way between the two extremes. She hoped that all men would be able to find a home in her Church. As we shall see, she was to be disappointed.

THE YOUNG HISTORIAN

1 Write extracts from a diary which might have been kept by the Vicar of Bray during (i) Aske's rebellion; (ii) the Marian persecution (*pic. 2*); and (iii) the debate over the Elizabethan Settlement, 1559. (Make sure that you use the correct dates for your extracts.)

2 Make a summary of the Elizabethan Settlement and then write a criticism of it which might have appeared in (i) a Catholic, and (ii) a Protestant newspaper.

3 Explain the importance of the part played by the owners of former monastic lands during the Elizabethan period (*pics. 4, 10, 14 and 16* will help you.)

4 Give an account of the clash between the Lords and the Commons in 1559 as might have appeared in letters written from London by (i) a Catholic and (ii) a Protestant extremist.

5 Write the headlines which might have appeared above reports of the activities of magistrates in (i) a Catholic area such as Hereford and (ii) a more Protestant area such as East Anglia.

6 Give an account which a visitor to London might have written on seeing Elizabeth make her way to a meeting of her Parliament (*pic. 22*).

7 Make a collage of headlines which might have appeared about the religious problems during the reigns of Henry VIII, Edward VI, Queen Mary and Queen Elizabeth.

8 Make a copy of the signature of Queen Elizabeth (*pic. 24*). You may want to decorate it.

5 Elizabethan Catholics

Elizabeth's hopes

As the young Queen, surrounded by her courtiers (*pic. 40*), rode to one or other of her palaces (*pic. 25*), she must have hoped that her religious settlement would bring peace to her people and country. While the Act of Uniformity insisted that everyone should attend Sunday Service in their parish church, it did allow those who had "a reasonable excuse" to stay away; people who could not satisfy the local magistrate with their excuse were fined twelve pence each time they were summoned and found guilty of non-attendance. This was not a great sum of money for the wealthy landowning Catholics of the North and West, and in any case many magistrates did not send out summonses against their Catholic neighbours.

Elizabeth's treatment of Catholics and extremist Protestants was very

25 Nonsuch Palace, at Cheam in Surrey, was conveniently placed near other royal palaces at Hampton, Kew, Richmond and London, and it was a royal favourite for "there was non such as pleasant". As can be seen from this picture, hunting was a popular pastime at Nonsuch.

lenient compared to the way in which European rulers treated people who differed from them in religion. There was to be no burning of heretics, no execution of religious opponents, and no persecution of people for their beliefs — or so she hoped.

Catholic opposition

But as the Queen rode around the country, she passed the ruins of hundreds of monasteries. These had been among the centres of the Catholic faith until they had been destroyed during Henry VIII's reign. And many of the important Catholic families still remembered "the old religion" and "the old ways" when monks sang in what were now "ruined choirs". These Catholics would not be satisfied until their religion was fully restored.

Other Catholic families were angered by the way in which "new men" had taken the places once occupied by the older nobility, many of whom were still Catholics. Great lords such as Arundel and Norfolk, Northumberland and Westmorland, Percy and Neville, knew that their ancestors had once acted as advisers to Kings. Now they saw their places taken by Cecils (*pic. 16*), Dudley (*pic. 9*), Raleigh (*pic. 10*) and other ambitious men "on the make". Some of these Catholics plotted with Mary, Queen of Scots, in 1569 to overthrow Elizabeth, in order to marry Mary to Norfolk and so re-establish Catholicism in England.

The Rising, 1569

The Earl of Northumberland's father had been executed after Aske's rising in 1536. In 1569 he called on his tenants and their families to follow him into a war against Cecil and Elizabeth. He and the other great landowners raised a large army and won the support of Yorkshire farmers with their banner of Christ's Five Wounds. They had a Mass said in Durham Cathedral and supervised the burning of Church of England prayer books as they marched triumphantly through the villages of the North and as far as Selby in Yorkshire.

But their triumph was short-lived. The Protestant government of Scotland sent an army south to help Elizabeth, whose own forces moved up from London to chase the rebels back to the North. Some escaped over the border into Scotland; others were defeated in battle, and when the fighting ended some eight hundred leading Catholics were executed.

The uncertain men

There is some evidence that Leicester (*pic. 9*) and other courtiers planned to support the Catholic rising — in the hope that this would lead, at least, to the fall of Cecil and Walsingham. As we have seen (page 20), Leicester's protégé, Essex, did, in fact, lead just such an anti-Cecil rising in 1601.

But Leicester and his friends did not rise in 1569. In France a cynical Protestant, Henry of Navarre, later became a Catholic so that he could win the throne of France. His famous phrase was: "Paris is worth a Mass". Maybe Leicester and his friends, such as the Earl of Southampton, thought that their new lands and wealth were "worth" the new religious settlement. Perhaps, too, they

26 King Philip of Spain and Queen Mary I, the last Catholic Tudor monarch. Notice the rich clothing, the tapestries on the walls and the coats of arms — some evidence of Tudor interest in heraldry.

remembered the ways in which the last Catholic Queen, Mary (*pic. 26*), had tried to impose her religion on the country and how this had led to widespread persecution and unrest. Leicester, Raleigh and the rest wanted a united country, able to stand up to Spain. A Catholic Queen, like Mary of Scotland, might have divided the country and so prevented the expansion of trade and industry which the "new men" hoped for.

Excommunication

In May 1570 the Pope, Pius V, issued a declaration that Elizabeth was to be regarded as a heretic, and that she was no longer to be considered rightful ruler of England. This announcement came too late for the rebels who had, by now, been executed. If it had come earlier, maybe many others would have joined their attempt to throw Elizabeth off the throne. What the Pope's decision did mean, however, was that Catholics in England need no longer feel duty-bound to obey Elizabethan laws; indeed the Pope condemned all those who did obey such heretical laws.

This announcement angered Cecil and Elizabeth's other Protestant advisers. They were even more angry when they discovered another plot in 1571: Catholics proposed to assassinate Elizabeth and to put Mary, Queen of Scots, on the throne. Then in 1572 they heard of the way in which the French Catholic Queen-Mother, Catherine de Medici, had ordered her troops to massacre the leading Protestant French nobles who had been brought to Paris for the wedding of their leader, Prince Henry of Navarre, to the young French King's sister. This massacre took place on St Bartholomew's Day (24 August) 1572. The Pope and the Spanish King Philip welcomed the news of the deaths of some eight thousand French Protestants. Elizabeth and her Protestant advisers were horrified at it — and frightened that English Catholics might behave similarly if they had their way and managed to put a Catholic monarch on the English throne.

Recusants

Most of the ordinary people in England accepted Elizabeth's religious settlement. The majority of parish clergy imitated the Vicar of Bray and followed the new prayer book and the services ordered by Elizabeth and her moderate Archbishop of Canterbury, Matthew Parker.

Most of the richer people also gave up their Catholicism and went, as ordered, to their parish churches. In great houses such as Hardwick Hall (*pic. 27*) services were said in English, on the orders of ambitious landowners who were anxious to keep favour with their Queen and to increase their wealth and comfort.

And yet there were a small number of Catholic families who refused to attend the new services. Some of these recusants (from the Latin verb "recusare" — to refuse) moved from their homes when the local magistrates ordered that

38

"Communion had to be taken according to the new way" at Easter time. Others were more fortunate where friendly magistrates did not trouble them with summonses or insist on church attendance. In the great homes of such families there were priests who still said the Latin Mass — attended by the family and their friends. At first Elizabeth and her Ministers did not move against these people. They hoped that in time such families would die out and the Catholic religion thus disappear.

European-trained priests

There were no colleges for training Catholic priests in Elizabethan England. In 1568 an Englishman, William Allen, founded such a college (or *seminary*) at Douai in Flanders; later he moved it to Rheims, and also founded another English College in Rome.

27   Hardwick Hall, Derbyshire, was built in the 1590s by the famous Bess of Hardwick. She married her first husband when she was only twelve years old; when she was twenty-seven she married Sir William Cavendish, who made a fortune as a courtier-politician. Bess inherited his property and wealth in 1577, and in 1580 she married an even greater courtier whose wealth she inherited when he died in 1565. In 1568 she married the Earl of Shrewsbury who owned seven great homes to add to the four which Bess already owned. She was the richest woman in England and then set about building this gigantic home — a monument to the success of some people in making money in Tudor England.

In these colleges abroad young Englishmen were trained as priests prepared to go back into England where they could say Mass for the remaining Catholics, and try to win back others to the "old religion". By 1580 there were over a hundred such Douai-trained priests at work in England.

In that year the Pope approved a new venture. Two Englishmen, Edmund Campion and Robert Parsons, had joined a recently founded religious order, the Society of Jesus, or the Jesuits. Fathers Campion and Parsons returned to England in 1580 not only to serve the remaining Catholics but to win back the country for the Pope and Catholicism.

Cecil and Walsingham saw these Jesuits as much more than religious fanatics. They were, said the Protestant politicians, part of a Spanish plot to overthrow Elizabeth so that Mary of Scotland could be put on the throne. In 1581 Campion was captured in Berkshire. He was tortured on the rack and executed on the grounds that he was opposed to Elizabeth's rule and was therefore a traitor — although he claimed he was a loyal subject of the Queen. Parsons had a printing press which Walsingham's spies tracked down to Essex. It was closed down, but Parsons escaped capture and fled to the Continent.

The anti-Catholic campaign

Now began the anti-Catholic campaign which was to last for three hundred years. By the end of Elizabeth's reign, about two hundred Catholics had been executed while many more had been imprisoned for life. The fine for failure to attend parish churches was increased to £20 a month; anyone caught attending a Mass in secret could be fined and imprisoned; anyone converted from being a Protestant to being a Catholic or anyone trying to persuade someone to do so could be declared a traitor, and be punished with hanging and quartering.

Catholics argued then and still claim that this was an anti-religious campaign in which the victims were punished for their religious beliefs. Elizabeth and her advisers argued that such people were allies of the Pope (who had declared her unfit to rule), of Spain (which tried to invade England in 1588) and of Mary, Queen of Scots. Cecil, Walsingham and the rest argued that national unity required religious uniformity; all those who disagreed with the religious settlement were treated as political rebels — much the same as dissenters are treated in modern Russia.

The Catholics and Essex

We have seen that in 1600 the ambitious Essex tried to lead a rising against Robert Cecil and the aging Queen. Among the leaders in Essex's plot were the men who, in 1605, were to organize the Gunpowder Plot. This did not happen until James Stuart had become King James I of England, but the unrest shown by the Essex plot and rising was an early sign that Elizabeth's policies had not had the total success she had hoped for. Furthermore, if her last years were marred by the Catholic plots, they were also burdened with the knowledge that some extremist Protestants were equally dissatisfied with her *via media*. The seeds of the religious struggles and Civil War of the seventeenth century were sown during Elizabeth's reign although they did not come to fruition until after her death.

THE YOUNG HISTORIAN

1 Write the letter which might have been sent by a Catholic nobleman living near a ruined monastery. (He might have written about the ways in which some "new families" had become rich out of former monastic land, the hopes he had had during the reign of Queen Mary and his anger at Elizabeth's religious settlement.)

2 Write the letter which a Catholic noble might have written to explain why he was unwilling to support the rising of 1569.

3 Write the letters which might have been exchanged between a recusant and one of the families which decided to conform to Elizabeth's settlement (*pic. 27* might give some ideas on why such conforming took place).

4 Write the account which might have appeared about the meeting of Elizabeth and her Ministers when they discussed the work of Fathers Campion and Parsons. (What might Elizabeth have said about the Pope's declaration of 1570; about the rising of 1569; and about the ways in which she had tried to help Catholics in her settlement? What would Cecil have said about the dangers from Spain; from Mary, Queen of Scots; and about the assassination plots? What would Walsingham have said about the evidence produced by his spies in Europe; of the work of his torturers; and of the treacherous behaviour of recusants?)

5 Explain why Catesby and other Catholics supported Essex's plot in 1600.

6 Write the headlines which might have appeared above reports of (i) the visit of Elizabeth I to a local palace such as Nonsuch (*pic. 25*); (ii) the start of the rising of 1569 — in Catholic, Protestant, Spanish and Scottish newspapers; (iii) the failure of the rising — in those same newspapers; (iv) the Pope's declaration of 1570 — in Catholic and Protestant newspapers; (v) the St Bartholomew's Day Massacre in Paris — in Catholic and Protestant newspapers; (vi) the founding of the English College at Douai.

7 Give an account of Campion's mission, arrest, trial and execution, as it might have appeared in newspapers owned by (i) a Catholic; (ii) a Protestant; (iii) a government Minister; (iv) Philip of Spain.

8 Paint or draw your own version of "A rich lady".

9 Make the posters which might have been issued by (i) Northumberland appealing to his tenants in 1569, and (ii) Walsingham asking for information about the work of Jesuits and other priests after 1580.

6 Elizabeth and Mary Stuart, Queen of Scots

The question of the succession

We have seen that one of the main problems facing Elizabeth I was that of her own marriage. She and her Ministers realized that, if she did not have children, the next claimant to the throne was Mary Stuart, Queen of Scots (*pic. 28*). She had become Queen of Scots when she was only one week old; her father, King James V of Scotland, had been killed fighting Henry VIII's army at the Battle of Solway Moss.

Henry had offered to call off his war against the Scots on condition that the Scottish nobles and Parliament agreed to a marriage between his son and heir, the future Edward VI, and the still-infant Mary. This was in line with the policy of Henry VII, the previous English King, who had married his daughter Margaret Tudor to James IV of Scotland. After Henry VIII's death, the Protector Somerset continued the war against the Scots in the hope of forcing them to agree to this marriage proposal.

Mary and the French

For many years the French had been allies of the Scots — both of them being enemies of the English. In 1547 this alliance was strengthened by the marriage of Mary to the Dauphin of France — the heir to the French throne.

When Queen Mary of England (Mary Tudor) died in 1558, many Catholics thought of Mary of Scotland as the real Queen; they did not believe that Elizabeth should become Queen because she was the daughter of Henry VIII's

28   The Stuart claim to the English throne.

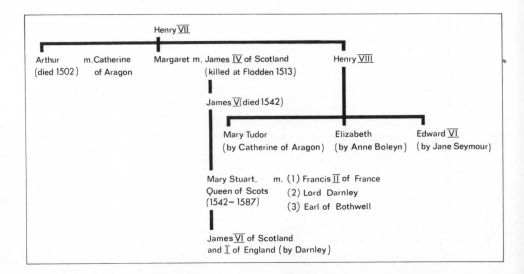

42

marriage to Anne Boleyn which had never been recognized by the Church. The French were eager to support Mary's claim. But Philip of Spain, enemy to the French, was opposed to it even though it would have meant a Catholic England. For him it was still better that England be under the Protestant Elizabeth than Catholic but linked to Scotland and France. This helps to explain why Philip did nothing to try to throw Elizabeth off the throne for the first thirty years of her reign.

Mary and the Scots

The young Queen Mary of Scots was taken to France to marry and live with the French Dauphin, while her French mother, Mary of Guise, lived in Scotland, acting as Regent on her behalf. She annoyed the Scottish Protestants, led by John Knox (*pic. 30*). At the same time Mary's husband became King of France on the death of his father in 1559 — and so she stayed in France.

Unfortunately for her, the King died in 1560 and the next French government did not want Mary to stay on in France. In 1561, therefore, she returned to her native Scotland to reign in her own right. She was a fervent Catholic but allowed her Protestant people to follow their own religion. This made her popular while her charming manners and good looks made her at first a well-loved Queen.

Mary and marriage

But Mary was not as wise and cautious as her cousin, Elizabeth of England. Instead of being content as Queen of Scotland, she seemed to be trying to

29 Mary Stuart, Queen of Scots, drawn by the French painter François Clouet just before her return to Scotland after the death of her first husband.

30 John Knox, Scotland's leading reformer and vigorous opponent of Mary's Catholicism.

IOANNES CNOXVS.

strengthen her claims also to the English throne. Elizabeth realized the danger of this for her own position, and so she sent a Catholic nobleman, Henry Stuart, Lord Darnley, to propose marriage to the Catholic Queen of Scots. He was English and was also Mary's cousin; like Mary he was a descendant of Margaret Tudor. He appeared to be a charming man, fit to be the husband of the Catholic claimant to the English throne (*pic. 31*). In fact, he was a thoroughly unstable man who provided his queenly wife with none of the affection or love that she had hoped for. It is probable that Elizabeth had known Darnley's true character and sent him to Mary in the hope that she would foolishly allow herself to be trapped into this unworthy marriage.

Mary soon quarrelled with Darnley. She gave her love and friendship to her Italian secretary, David Rizzio. Darnley then complained to the Scottish Protestant lords, promising that if they helped him get rid of Rizzio he would see to it that they enjoyed even greater freedom and power than the Catholic Queen Mary was willing to allow them. As a result, one night in the spring of 1566, Darnley let some of the Protestant lords into Queen Mary's private rooms where they seized Rizzio and put him to death (*pic. 53*).

31 Darnley and his younger brother, painted two years before Darnley's marriage to his cousin, Mary Stuart. Notice the panelling along the walls, the beams in the ceiling and the leaded windows of this Elizabethan hall.

Mary and Bothwell

For a short time after Rizzio's death Mary seemed to have been reconciled to Darnley; she even nursed him when he had smallpox. In fact, she was involved in an affair with a brutal and reckless Scottish noble, the Earl of Bothwell (*pic. 32*). Early in 1567 she persuaded Darnley to move to a house outside Edinburgh called Kirk o' Fields — where she said he would have more chance of recovering from his smallpox. A few weeks after his arrival, she left him there to go to a party at Holyrood Palace in Edinburgh. While she was at the party, it is thought that Bothwell led a gang who blew up the house. Darnley was not killed in the explosion; his dead body was discovered in the garden where he had been attacked and killed.

Instead of punishing Bothwell for his probable part in this murder, Mary allowed him and his warlike followers to impose their will on the Court of Inquiry set up to investigate Darnley's death. She then arranged that Bothwell should "kidnap" her, and issued a statement in which she said that "her honour" required that she should marry her captor. Having helped to arrange a divorce for her "kidnapper", she married him a few days later.

Mary to England

Mary's behaviour angered almost everyone in Scotland. The Protestant nobles formed an army which outnumbered the Queen's troops, and Mary was captured by them at Carberry Hill. Bothwell escaped to Denmark where he died some years later as a lunatic chained to a pillar in a dungeon.

The Scottish Protestants tried to persuade Mary to renounce her marriage to Bothwell. She refused to do so. They then imprisoned her in Lochleven Castle, which stood in the middle of a lake. They forced her to sign a document in which she agreed to give up the throne in favour of her (and Darnley's) infant son, James Stuart, who was declared James VI of Scotland.

Mary escaped from prison, raised a small army and tried to win back her throne. But her army was defeated by a Protestant army led by her half-brother, the Earl of Moray. Mary rode from the battlefield on a ninety-mile

32 The only known portrait of Bothwell.

45

journey to England. Here she asked for the support and help of her cousin, Elizabeth. Would Elizabeth help her to win back her throne? No. Would Elizabeth allow her to make her way to France where she might get other help? No.

Mary and the English plotters

Some of Elizabeth's Protestant advisers wanted her to put Mary on trial for the murder of Darnley and then have her executed. They saw Mary as a threat to their own Queen's safety. But Elizabeth was wiser than Walsingham and others. She saw that while Mary was alive, but in prison, the Spanish King would not move against England — for he would not want to have a French sympathizer on the throne of England. So, for nineteen years Mary was kept in one prison-castle after another.

In 1569 the Catholic nobles of Northern England planned to have Mary married to the Duke of Norfolk and to raise an army, in order to force Elizabeth to help Mary regain her throne in Scotland and acknowledge her as the rightful heir to the throne of England. Mary went even further than this. She wrote to Philip of Spain asking for his help in overthrowing Elizabeth so that Mary might be "Queen of England within three months so that Mass would be said all over the country".

But Philip did not send help. And Walsingham's spies knew all about the plot. Norfolk was arrested and the other leaders told to report to the Queen in London. We have seen that, having refused to obey that order, they rose in rebellion which ended in disaster (Chapter 5).

There were many other plots which came to nothing — owing to the work of Walsingham's secret service and the stupidity of some of Mary's supporters who were not able to organize things properly. But in 1586 Walsingham's men played a part in encouraging and then exposing a more serious plot led by an English Catholic, Anthony Babington. Indeed, Walsingham's men carried the letters between Mary and Babington in which they planned the assassination of Elizabeth so that Mary could ascend to the throne.

Mary's trial and execution

Walsingham waited until he had in his hands a letter in which Mary approved the plot. Then he arrested the plotters, exposed their scheme and had Babington tried and executed.

He, and many others, asked that Mary Stuart should also be put to death. Elizabeth was opposed to this. She feared the anger in Scotland, France and Spain if the beautiful Catholic Queen were to be executed. But she was forced to allow Mary to be put on trial. When Mary was found guilty, Elizabeth very reluctantly signed the document for Mary's execution. But she did ask that the warrant of execution should not be sent off until arrangements had been made for Mary's death to take place privately rather than as a public execution.

Cecil, Walsingham and the other Protestant advisers would not wait. They feared that while Mary lived there was always a danger of a Catholic rising in her favour. They sent off the warrant without telling their Queen and on 7 February 1587 Mary Stuart was executed at Fotheringay Castle in Northamptonshire.

And after her death?

Elizabeth was very angry when she was told of the execution — or at least she claimed to be. She ordered a state funeral for her dead cousin, claiming that the execution was "a mistake". Catholics saw in the dead Queen a martyr for their religion. They hoped that her son, James VI — and the next claimant to the English throne — would honour his mother's memory by restoring Catholicism

33 The execution of Mary, Queen of Scots on 8 February 1587 at Fotheringay Castle. The drawing shows three stages of the procedure: the Queen enters (left), is prepared (centre) and is executed (right of centre).

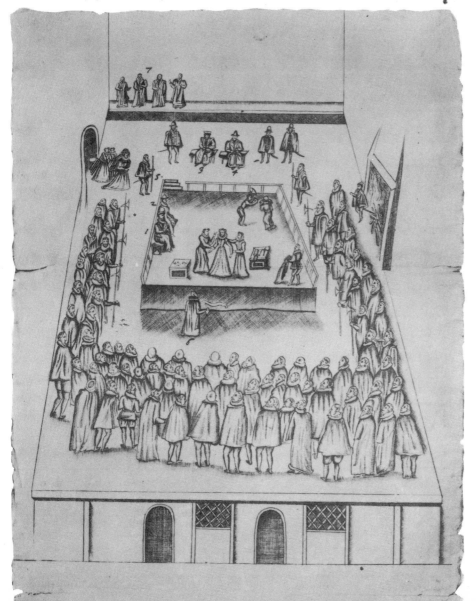

in England. His failure to do so was one cause of the Gunpowder Plot.

Philip of Spain must have welcomed the news of Mary's death. For this allowed him to put forward his own claim to the throne as the King-husband of Queen Mary I (*pic. 26*). It also freed him from worry that the English throne might go to a Queen sympathetic to the French. Mary was executed in 1587. Philip's Great Armada sailed to invade England at the first suitable opportunity. If Mary had not been killed in 1587 there might possibly never have been the Armada of 1588.

THE YOUNG HISTORIAN

1 Write the headlines which might have appeared in newspapers owned by (i) an English Catholic, (ii) an English Protestant, (iii) the French government, (iv) the Spanish government, (v) a supporter of John Knox and (vi) a Scottish Catholic about: (a) Queen Mary's return to Scotland in 1561, (b) Mary's marriage to Darnley, (c) the death of Rizzio, (d) Mary's flight to England, and (e) her execution. (You might make a collage of headlines for each of these events and then write a note explaining why different papers carried differing sorts of headlines.)

2 Write the letter in which an English Catholic might have explained his support for Mary's claim to the English throne (*pic. 28*).

3 Write the report which the Spanish Ambassador in London (*pic. 13*) might have sent to Philip II, arguing against helping Mary, Queen of Scots, in 1569.

4 Write the letter which might have been sent by a Scot who was angered by Mary's marriage to Bothwell.

5 Write the letter which the Spanish Ambassador might have sent to Philip II after the death of Queen Mary. How might that letter have differed from the one sent in 1569 (question 3)?

6 Write extracts from a diary which might have been kept by Walsingham (*pic. 17*), concerning his fears about the campaign against Mary and other opponents of Elizabeth I.

7 Paint or draw the posters which might have been used to advertize (i) the execution of Anthony Babington, (ii) the state funeral of Queen Mary.

8 Paint or draw Mary, Queen of Scots (*pic. 29*).

9 Make up your own version of the death warrant (*pic. 12*) for Queen Mary. You might use Elizabeth I's signature (*pic. 24*). Sprinkle your "warrant" with drops of vinegar and roll it up, tie it with ribbon and put it in a hot oven for a few minutes. This will give it a "document-like" dried-out and yellowed look.

7 Elizabeth and the Puritans

The ordinary people and the religious question

When Elizabeth came to the throne her most serious problem was that of religion. But for the ordinary people the main problem was that of making a living. And while Elizabeth and her Ministers argued about the religious settlement, most Englishmen got on with their work as farmers or farmworkers. The ploughman in his rough clothing guided his clumsy wooden machine behind the teams of horses or oxen (*pic. 34*). Other men and women used heavy wooden hammers to break up the soil ready for raking and for sowing the seeds. At harvest time everyone in the village joined in the haymaking and gathering of the corn crops. If God had been kind, the people would eat well during the winter; if the harvest had been bad, people were close to starving — and many died.

So, ordinary men and women had not the time or the knowledge to get involved in the great religious arguments. While the men laboured in the fields, the women also worked on the land, span and wove the cloth (*pic. 35*), and ran their homes.

34 A village scene from a Tudor manuscript.

The rich and the religious question

Many of the better-off people had the time and intelligence to take an interest in the religious debates — if they wanted to. Many chose not to get involved. Often the new landowners spent their time making sure that they got an increasing income from their estates. Merchants and traders looked after their businesses. Such men were more anxious about their life on earth than about life after death. Their large homes (*pic. 36*) were more important to them than the way in which the local clergy ran the church services.

Extremist Protestants

There were, as we have seen, a small number of people anxious to bring back Catholicism. And there were also a small number who wanted to make the English Church even more Protestant and much less like the Catholic Church than Elizabeth wished. Elizabeth's settlement established a Church in which there was a Supreme Governor, archbishops, bishops, and local clergy who wore richly decorated vestments to say the various services. All this was much like the Catholic Church — and like the Lutheran Church in Germany.

But a Frenchman, John Calvin, had set up another sort of church, with its headquarters in Geneva in Switzerland. Calvin wanted his church to be like the early Christian church, when there had been no Pope in Rome, no Kings as Supreme Governors and no bishops. Calvin wanted the people in each of his local churches to elect *presbyters* or elders who would organize the work of their local church. The members of the church would also elect their own minister and, if there were many churches in an area or county, they would elect a governing body for the church as a whole.

35 Women spinning and weaving. This picture is from a fifteenth-century manuscript and the ordinary women in Elizabethan times would not have been as well-dressed as this.

36 Scarisbrick, one of the many large manor houses built during the Tudor period. These houses, their furniture and leaded windows were the outward signs of the wealth, ambitions and expectations of English landowners and merchants.

50

In Elizabeth's Church of England, as in the Catholic Church, the most important service was Communion or the Mass. But in Calvin's church the most important thing was the sermon (*pic. 37*) in which the minister would explain the Scripture to the people — who were then told to go away to study it for themselves in organized meetings or in their own homes.

Englishmen and Calvin

There was no chance for the ordinary Englishman to find out about the work of John Calvin in Switzerland or the ways in which his ideas spread in France, the Netherlands and other parts of Europe. But some Englishmen did travel abroad and learn about this new church. For example, scholars from the Universities of Oxford and Cambridge went to study at European Universities. Some of them brought back news about Calvin's church; others brought back books and pamphlets in which the ideas of Calvin were explained. And it was from the Universities that there came a demand that the English Church should be made less like the Catholic Church and still more Protestant. These extremists asked that the Church should be "purified" from traces of Catholicism — and they became known as Puritans. They objected to ministers wearing vestments, to organ music being played during services, and to the use of candles on the altar. They could not find any mention of such things in the Scriptures — and they wanted to ban them.

Traders, seamen and Calvin

But it was not only scholars who went abroad. An increasing number of Englishmen were involved in foreign trade; sailors, merchants and traders went into Europe as part of their work and they, too, learned about Calvin's church. And they liked what they saw. They liked the idea of electing the elders to control the work of the local church, and the idea of choosing their own minister instead of having one sent by a bishop appointed by the Queen.

The argument followed: if they were allowed to choose the minister who preached their religion, why should they not choose the politicians and rulers who ran their country? After all, religion (and the fate of their souls) was more important than trade and other activities which would end (for them)

when they died. And if they were fit to choose the people who ran the more important part of their lives, they were obviously fit to choose the people who ran the less important part.

So in the sea ports and market towns (*pic. 38*) there was growing support for the Puritan idea.

Presbyterians

University scholars, merchants and country gentlemen supported the small number of the clergy who wanted to do away with bishops and their power to appoint ministers, and to hand that power over to local congregations. But the bishops were chosen by the Queen and were the chief way in which she could control the Church throughout the country. It is not surprising, therefore, that the Queen was opposed to the Presbyterians.

Independents

Other Puritans wanted to go even further. They were opposed to any general system of Church government. They wanted each local congregation to be independent under its own elected minister. These Puritans were first called Brownists — because their leader was a Robert Browne. Later, in Stuart times, they became known as Independents and later still in English history they were called Congregationalists.

The Bible and good works

But all the Puritans agreed on many things. They thought, for example, that each man could discover God's truth by studying the Scriptures (*pic. 39*),

37 A plainly dressed minister addresses his congregation.

although they admitted that this study would be better done after instruction from a learned minister (*pic. 37*).

They also agreed that they ought to show in their daily lives that they were God's elect, or chosen ones. This led them to avoid all the vanities of the ordinary world such as richly decorated clothes. They tried to use God's time wisely — by working hard — and not waste it in idle things such as gambling, drinking or at theatres.

Elizabeth and the Puritans

Up until the later part of Elizabeth's reign the Puritans were not a great threat to the religious settlement. There were few of them and they were content to argue their case inside the Church which Elizabeth had set up. In 1583 Elizabeth appointed a new Archbishop of Canterbury, Whitgift, with instructions that he was to put down this Puritan movement inside the Church.

He tried to do so — in pamphlets and instructions to his clergy. He dismissed any clergy who were found to be putting Puritan ideas into practice in their local church. But this did not stamp out the growing movement. Indeed, the dismissed ministers set up their own churches; some people who continued to attend the local parish church would then go on to private Puritan services for prayers and discussion. And in their discussions they found that they were becoming critical of the Elizabethan government which insisted on a non-Puritan church and which did not allow ordinary people a say about the running of their church or their government. We shall see in Chapter 8 that this led to the growth of a Puritan movement inside Parliament.

Elizabeth could not allow this challenge to her Church and her government. In 1593 anyone refusing to attend the local parish church or who was found guilty of attending unauthorized religious meetings could be sentenced to exile or to death. These measures were aimed at both Catholics and Puritans.

◄ **38** Exeter Guildhall, one sign of the growth of that market town during the Tudor period. It is worth noting that many of Elizabeth's supporters came from Devon and Cornwall where industry and trade — and Puritanism — grew rapidly.

39 The four evangelists (Matthew, Mark, Luke and John) stone the Pope. This painting was done in 1536 and represents the extreme Protestant view of the power of the Bible.

We have seen that some disappointed Catholics supported Essex's plot in 1600 and that in 1605 they took part in the Gunpowder Plot.

The Puritans waited patiently until James VI of Scotland came to the throne of England. They hoped that he would bring with him the ideas of Knox (*pic. 30*) and the Scottish Presbyterian Church. But James realized that if he allowed greater democracy in the Church this would lead to the demand for greater democracy in the political life of the country. "No bishops", he said, "no King". And he refused to allow the Puritans the freedom they had hoped for. It was some of these Puritans who sailed in the *Mayflower* to set up the first successful English colony in America. But that is part of the story of *The Stuart Age*.

THE YOUNG HISTORIAN

1 Explain why ordinary people (*pics. 34 and 35*) did not get involved in the religious debate.

2 Write extracts from a diary which might have been kept by a rich land-owner or merchant, showing how his standard of living improved in Elizabethan times. (You might use *pics. 4, 9, 10, 14, 15, 23, 27, and 36* to give you some ideas for extracts on buying clothes, furniture and building materials, his meetings with tailors, window-makers, heralds who were designing his coat of arms, and so on.)

3 Write the letter in which a University student might have explained to his parents how he has learnt about Calvinism and why he supports these extremist ideas. Write the reply in which his father warns him against opposing the Queen's religious settlement.

4 Make up the headlines which might have appeared above reports on (i) a congregation choosing its minister — in a government newspaper; (ii) a congregation dismissing a minister — in newspapers owned by (a) Puritans and (b) one of the Cecil family; (iii) the appointment of Whitgift — in newspapers owned by (a) Puritans and (b) moderate Protestants; (iv) the laws against Puritanism after 1593.

5 Write the article which might have appeared in a newspaper trying to explain to readers the main differences between Elizabeth's Anglican Church and the Church wanted by the Puritans. (The writer might have mentioned appointment and power of bishops, the importance of the Communion and the sermon, church music and ministers' clothing, the appointment of ministers.)

6 Explain why Puritanism was more common in the South West (*pic. 38*) than in the Northern counties.

7 Draw or paint the posters which might have been used to (i) invite Puritans to a meeting where they would choose a new minister, (ii) advertize the execution of a Puritan.

8 Elizabeth and her Parliaments

Elizabeth's problems

During the last ten years or so of her long reign Elizabeth I had to face many problems. There was the religious problem caused by the extremists among the Catholics and Puritans. There was the Essex rising in which Catholics played some part. This chapter will examine another problem — that caused by the growth of power of the House of Commons (*pic. 22*).

The growth of Parliamentary influence

Elizabeth's grandfather, Henry VII, would not have understood the problem that Parliament caused for his granddaughter. He had only called Parliament to meet whenever he wanted money — and he had been careful not to spend too much. And so there were few Parliaments during his reign.

But Elizabeth's father, Henry VIII, had called Parliament often in the 1530s — not because he needed money, but because he wanted them to pass the laws which would allow him to make the break with the Roman Catholic Church, set up his own Church, divorce Catherine of Aragon, marry Anne Boleyn and seize the property of the monasteries. There were regular meetings of Parliament and, as a result, Members of Parliament got to know each other well, began to realize that the King depended on their support and so began to get an idea of their own importance.

The "new men" and Parliament

Elizabeth surrounded herself with a band of young, rich and ambitious courtiers (*pic. 40*). Some of these men came from families which had become rich as a result of grants of land taken from the Catholic monks and nuns. Such were the Sidney family who lived at Penshurst as the family home, the Wriothesleys who lived at Beaulieu, the Bacons at Gorhambury, the Thynnes at Longleat (*pic. 14*) and the Dudleys (*pic. 9*).

But among Elizabeth's supporters were men from families which were still trying to make their mark and their fortune. Raleigh (*pic. 10*), Drake (*pic. 48*), Hawkins and Gilbert were typical of the merchants, traders, sailors and explorers who looked to Elizabeth for their source of wealth.

Hawkins, Raleigh, Drake and Gilbert had several things in common — apart from their ambition. They all came from Devon or Cornwall and were all sailors, and all of them were Members of Parliament for various constituencies in the South West. As we have seen, Puritanism was very important in that area, and the four men shared a sympathy with these extremist Protestants.

Few Parliaments — and then more

Like Henry VII and Henry VIII, Elizabeth I was expected to "live of her own" — out of the income she received from her own lands, from fines paid at one or other of the many royal courts, from customs duties given for life by her first Parliament and from various payments which had to be made by her noble subjects. And for many years Elizabeth managed to "live of her own". She did not need more money and did not need to call Parliament to meet, to discuss requests for increased taxation. She spent little on food for her court, since she lived off the land in one or other of her palaces (*pic. 25*) or in one or other of the castles and country houses of her richer subjects (*pics. 3, 14 and 27*). She was careful to avoid spending money on war — until driven to do so in the 1570s and 1580s.

It was this spending on war which forced Elizabeth to ask Parliament for more taxation. Four times after 1587 Parliament was called to discuss the Queen's request for money — and, after a debate, gave her what she wanted. Like most of their countrymen, the Members of Parliament did not want to

40 Elizabeth I in procession to Blackfriars, London, with some of her courtiers. Notice the dress of the ladies and the men.

41 A small detail from the ► ceiling of the Long Gallery in Blickling Hall, Norfolk. Such fine work was a sign not only of the great ability of English workmen, but also of the wealth of the families who could afford to have the work done.

see Spain invading England and bringing back Catholicism. This would have meant the loss of their lands, removal from their homes where they enjoyed the comfort and pleasure of a well-designed and well-decorated house.

But the fact that even "Gloriana" (*pics. 8, 18 and 40*) had to ask for their permission to raise taxes gave Members of Parliament a sense of their own importance. Some of them even began to think that they might be as important as Elizabeth's Ministers and officials. In 1591 Peter Wentworth went so far as to claim that Parliament had the right to discuss and debate the question of Elizabeth's successor, the nature of the Elizabethan Church, and any other matters of Church or State that any member wanted to bring up. This was too much for the majority of MPs, who were still learning to enjoy their power

and did not know how to use it. Wentworth's claims were also too much for the Queen who had him arrested in 1593 and imprisoned in the Tower of London.

Parliament and monopolies

Elizabeth did not have the money to pay for the expeditions which the adventurous sailors made to various parts of the world. Raleigh, Drake, Gilbert and the rest had to spend their own money on fitting out and arming ships, paying sailors and stocking their ships with food and other necessities. One way in which she could encourage such adventurers — and other members of her Court — was to give them a monopoly (the sole right) to make, import or sell a certain article.

Sometimes there was a good case for such a monopoly. When a group of merchants put their money at risk to fit out ships to sail in search of trade in India, Russia, Turkey or Africa, it seemed fair that the Queen should encourage them by agreeing that, if they were successful, only they would be allowed to trade with the region which they had been the first to develop. Similarly, it seemed fair for an industrialist who had spent time and money on developing a new way of making glass (*pic. 42*) to be given the sole right to make such glass — at least for some years — so that he could make a profit from his efforts.

But other grants of monopolies were obviously unfair. Raleigh had the sole right to make and sell playing-cards; others had the monopoly over the salt trade. Indeed, when a list of such grants was read out in Parliament, one MP

42 The Drawing Room in Broughton Malherbe. Notice the seat in the window and the window itself with its leaded panes and coats-of-arms. Life was very comfortable in such homes — for mother and child.

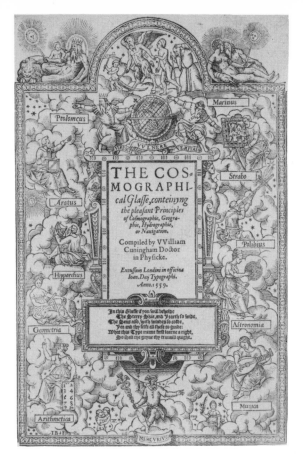

43 The title page of one of the many books printed during Elizabeth I's reign. The development of the printing press meant that people could enjoy reading and that religious tracts and pamphlets could be produced for wide distribution.

44 An Englishwoman of the Tudor middle classes. You might compare her clothing with that of the richer ladies in *pic. 40*.

shouted in mockery: "Is not bread there?" Those MPs who had been given such a grant did not see anything wrong with the system — which made them rich. Nor did the Queen see anything wrong in it — she was able to reward her favourites and also receive extra income out of the payments she forced them to make to her in return.

A new development

There is a danger that we might think that Elizabethan men in their tights and corsets were soft, gentle creatures. In fact, these were the men who defeated the Armada, sailed with Drake around the world and opened up new lands for their successors to develop and colonize. They were also more educated than their ancestors had been. The development of the printing press (*pic. 43*) and the enlargement of the Universities had given more men the opportunity to become well-read and educated.

This was one reason for the great confidence of the MPs in the last years of Elizabeth's reign. In 1591 Elizabeth became angry with Peter Wentworth, arguing that the only privilege the Commons had was to say "yea or no" with their reasons, "a liberal but not licentious speech", but that they could not "frame a form of religion or state of government" nor encroach on the powers of the Church, the succession, or royal policy.

In 1597-98 the Queen was forced to reject ten Bills put forward by her Parliament, while in 1601 Parliament was even angrier and more determined, "more fit for a grammar school", said Robert Cecil, "than a Court of Parliament" where the Commons "hawked, spat and hemmed". It was in this Parliament of 1601 that the Queen was forced to retreat in the face of the anger of the majority of MPs at the ways in which monopolies allowed a few to become rich. She claimed that she had never been a "grasper" or a "waster"; she withdrew most of the monopolies which she had only given, she said, "for lack of true information", although she claimed the "prerogative royal" to do as she wished.

Elizabeth did not call another Parliament in her remaining two years. She died in March 1603. The question of the relations between Parliament and the Crown was to dominate political life during the next century — *The Stuart Age*.

THE YOUNG HISTORIAN

1 Explain why the majority of members of the House of Lords supported Elizabeth I's religious policies.
2 Give an account of the opening of a new Parliament (*pic. 22*) which might have been written by a new member of the House of Commons from Exeter (*pic. 38*). Why were most MPs unwilling to challenge the Queen's policies?
3 Paint or draw "Elizabeth with some of her courtiers" (*pic. 40*).
4 Give a short account of a day in the life of *either* the husband *or* the wife in one of the country houses (*pics. 14 and 42*). (Such accounts might mention hunting, entertaining, riding, hawking, reading, servants, food supply, children, etc.)
5 Write the letter which might have been sent by a middle-class woman (*pics. 23 and 44*) who had gone to stay in a country house. (She might have written about the rich people's clothing, furniture and food and about the outdoor entertainment — *pic. 25*.)
6 The windows in *pic. 42* include some coats-of-arms. Make up a coat-of-arms for your own family with two, three or four sections to the shield. What part of your family's history would you wish to show in such a coat-of-arms? Why?
7 Paint or draw "An English gentleman" (*pics. 9 and 10*).

9 Elizabeth and Europe

A tangle of questions

When Elizabeth I came to the throne she faced a large number of problems, each of which was linked with the others. The question of her marriage affected the question of the attitudes of Spain and France towards England. The problem of religion could not be solved without affecting the attitude of Spain towards Elizabeth, particularly after the Pope's declaration of 1570.

The Hapsburgs and France

On the death of the Holy Roman Emperor Charles V, Europe's most powerful ruler, in 1558, his will showed that he divided his great Empire between his two sons. Ferdinand became the Emperor of Austria and ruler of Germany; Philip became King Philip II of Spain and of the Netherlands as well as ruler of parts of Italy.

The Valois Kings of France had felt threatened by the power of Charles V. For over thirty years their armies had marched against those of the Emperor

45 An army on the march. Notice the pikes carried by the foot soldiers, the armed cavalry, the clumsy carts which took the supplies for the army, the walled town which had to be besieged to force it to surrender, and the nature of the countryside through which the army marched — when the weather permitted.

(*pic. 45*). Thus, the unfortunate Emperor had been forced to fight against Catholic France while, at the same time, he was trying to stamp out the Protestant princes and other rulers of small German states who supported Martin Luther's demand for a reformation.

The French Kings took advantage of this religious division of the Austro-German Empire. But they were also faced with a strong and growing Protestant movement inside France. Here the Huguenots formed a threat to the power of the Valois.

Elizabeth and Europe

For over 300 years the rulers of England had claimed the right to rule parts of France, and throughout that period England and France had fought in a series of wars as the French Kings tried to win back the territories held by the English. England's ally had been Spain — which was often at war with France, in Italy and along the borders between Austria and France.

But Elizabeth and Cecil (*pic. 16*) realized that Philip of Spain was, in fact, England's most important enemy. His navies sailed the world's seas in search of a greater Empire (*pic. 46*) — and would be an obstacle to the English seamen and merchants who were anxious to expand English trade (*pic. 47*). They also knew that Philip was anxious to win back England for Catholicism and make Spain powerful over England. After all, that had been the reason for his marrying Mary Tudor (*pic. 26*) and for his proposal to Elizabeth in 1558.

So in 1559-60 Elizabeth and her Ministers made peace with France, giving up their claim to Calais, which had been the last English possession in that country. This did not mean that Elizabeth wanted to be friendly with France — where Mary Stuart was Queen after July 1559 and which was an ally of Catholic forces in Scotland. But it did bring England some peace, which saved money

46 A Spanish caravel sailing close to the wind, a painting by Pieter Brueghel, done in 1565. In such small ships the Spaniards, Portuguese and English sailors explored the world.

47 *The White Bear*, from an engraving by C.J. ► Visscher. Notice the guns in their port holes, the armed soldiers on deck and the sailor climbing above the stern of the ship to put a sail right.

and which gave Elizabeth a chance to get on with her religious settlement. Also, the Anglo-French peace caused Philip to hesitate to act against the Protestant Elizabeth. For, if he got rid of her, then, maybe, Mary Stuart would gain the throne (*pic. 28*).

A cold war against Spain, 1559-78

Philip of Spain sent an army to the Netherlands to try to stamp out Protestantism there. This invasion united nationalist-minded Catholics with the Dutch Protestants, and Philip found himself in a costly rebellion and war in the Netherlands. His Dutch opponents looked to Elizabeth for help against Spain. She allowed the ships of the "sea-beggars" (the name given to the rebels) to use Dover as a base where they could refit their ships, although she refused to send an army to help the rebels against Spain.

At the same time she was encouraging her seamen in their attempts to increase English trade. John Hawkins made three attempts to open up trade between England and the Spanish colonies in South America between 1562 and 1568. He bought or captured black slaves on the coast of West Africa and took them to the Spanish colonies where he sold them at a great profit. The Spanish planters welcomed such trade; but the Spanish government was opposed to Englishmen making a profit out of Spanish colonies. So in 1568 the Spanish attacked Hawkins's six ships at San Juan de Ulua (now known as Vera Cruz). Only two English ships escaped: the *Minion*, commanded by Hawkins, and the *Judith*. The Englishmen who were captured were hung by

their arms and given 200 lashes with whips before being taken to work as slaves. Hawkins and Drake (*pic. 48*), who had been commander of the *Judith,* had a hard time getting back to England and neither of them was willing to forget the Spaniards' savage treatment of Englishmen who were only trying to trade.

This helps to explain the way in which Drake plundered Spanish colonies during his journey round the world in 1577-80 (see Chapter 12). In 1572 he also led an attack on Spanish ports in Central America — this area was known as the Spanish Main by English sailors. With three ships Drake attacked ports in modern Panama, seized the gold intended for Spain and returned home a wealthy man.

Elizabeth and the Dutch rebels

In 1572 Catherine de Medici, the Queen-Mother of France, organized the St Bartholomew's Day Massacre (see page 38). Elizabeth and her Ministers were horrified at this and decided to send help to French Protestant rebels who had risen in anger in the South West of France. But Elizabeth was frightened that Catherine de Medici might now decide to help Mary, Queen of Scots, to gain the English throne. And so, in order to win Spanish friendship, she expelled the Dutch "sea-beggars" from Dover.

This forced them to take even firmer action in their own country. They seized the port of Brill, roused the people of Flushing and other ports along the Dutch coast to expel the Spaniards, and before long the four northern provinces

of the Netherlands were engaged in an all-out war, under the leadership of William the Silent (*pic. 49*).

Walsingham (*pic. 17*) wanted to declare an all-out war against Spain. Elizabeth refused to take such decisive action, even when her refusal forced William the Silent to ask for French help — for England did not want France to gain any great influence in the Netherlands. But Elizabeth saw that if France got involved this would increase the enmity between France and Spain — and it was becoming clear that Spain was England's main enemy. For about ten years (1576-85) Elizabeth's policy was, therefore, one of "prolonging and mincing" as Burghley said (*pic. 16*). She pretended to be still interested in the idea of a Spanish marriage and pointed to her refusal to help William as a sign that she was friendly to Spain — in spite of the attacks on Spanish colonies by her sea-dogs. At the same time she also suggested that she was interested in the idea of a marriage with the French heir, the Duke of Anjou, and encouraged French assistance to the Dutch rebels.

1585 — a year of decision

In June 1584 the Duke of Anjou died. This made the Protestant Henry of Navarre the next claimant to the French throne, and so it was certain that there would be a new religious war in France.

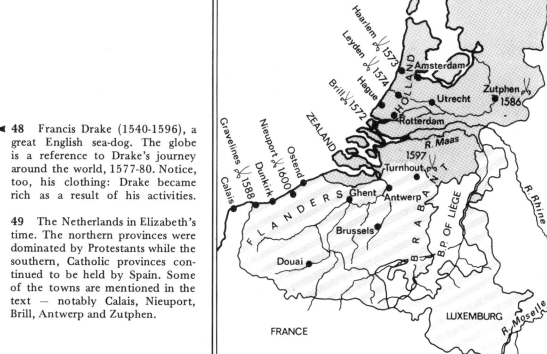

◄ **48**   Francis Drake (1540-1596), a great English sea-dog. The globe is a reference to Drake's journey around the world, 1577-80. Notice, too, his clothing: Drake became rich as a result of his activities.

49   The Netherlands in Elizabeth's time. The northern provinces were dominated by Protestants while the southern, Catholic provinces continued to be held by Spain. Some of the towns are mentioned in the text — notably Calais, Nieuport, Brill, Antwerp and Zutphen.

In the same month William the Silent was murdered. The Dutch rebels were deprived of their leader and in 1585 the Spanish re-took Antwerp. At the same time Philip of Spain signed an alliance with the Catholic leaders in France to make sure that there would not be a Protestant succession there.

English armies in the Netherlands
In 1585 Elizabeth decided to send an army of 6,000 men into the Netherlands to help the Dutch. This army was led by the Queen's aging favourite, Leicester (*pic. 9*). It was not well armed, nor was Leicester a good leader. The poet, Philip Sidney, died at the Battle of Zutphen — one of the few battles the English won.

Fortunately for English pride, the disasters of this land-war were over-shadowed by the exploits of Drake in his attacks on Vigo, Cartagena and Florida, from which he returned with £60,000 in loot and the knowledge that the Spaniards were not as strong as people feared.

The Armada
The death of Mary Stuart (*pic. 33*) removed the danger for Spain of a French sympathizer inheriting the English throne. Philip of Spain therefore decided to launch his great attack on England — in revenge for English attacks on his colonies and shipping, and for English help to the Dutch rebels.

In 1577 Elizabeth appointed John Hawkins Treasurer of her Navy Board. He organized the building of a new fleet of slimmer ships which were speedier and more manoeuvrable than previous ones. These ships carried as many guns as was possible at that time; an upper deck, or "gun deck", was added so that the heavy guns could still fire through port holes but leave room for storage below.

Spanish ships, on the other hand, were old-fashioned and not good for fighting. The main purpose of such ships was to carry soldiers for the invasion of enemy country — in the Netherlands, or in England.

In 1587 Drake led a fleet into the Spanish port of Cadiz where he sank, burnt or captured about thirty ships, took two forts near Cape St Vincent and seized a treasure ship near the Azores, all of which more than paid for the expedition. This "singeing of the King of Spain's beard" put off the sailing of the Armada and made Drake a popular hero when he returned to Plymouth — although the Queen had to pretend that she was annoyed with him for having disobeyed her orders.

The defeat of the Armada, July 1588
In July 1588 the great Armada finally sailed. The plan was that the 130 ships would carry their soldier-passengers through the English Channel where they were to link up with Spanish forces from the Netherlands, and so invade England.

To oppose this fleet England had a Royal Navy of about 40 ships plus another 150 privately-owned ones. Lord Howard of Effingham was commander of this array of ships — but he had the good sense to listen to the brilliant captains under his command, Hawkins, Drake and Frobisher.

The Spanish fleet sailed successfully into Calais. Then there was a change in the direction of the wind. It now blew from the southwest. The English sent fire-ships into the crowded anchorage. The Spaniards, who had not yet taken their troops on board, cut their mooring cables and set sail away from the fire. The freshening wind drove them along the Channel, closely followed

50   The "Armada Portrait" of Elizabeth I. Notice the dress, collar, jewellery, and the wig of the balding Queen. Her hand confidently rests on the globe; Englishmen had sailed around the world, and large parts of it would belong to England in later centuries. Notice, in the two panels, the reference to the Armada.

by English ships attacking them. The Spaniards then turned north, in the hope that they could sail to safety around the British Isles. But the speedier English ships sank some, poor seamanship led to others being wrecked, and only 55 of the great fleet returned home to a dispirited Spain (*pic. 50*).

The continuing war

But the defeat of the Armada did not end the fighting between Spain and England. Nor did England enjoy the continuing success that many must have hoped for. In 1589 thousands of English sailors died during Drake's unsuccessful raid on Spain and Portugal. In 1591 Sir Richard Grenville's *Revenge* was captured by a large Spanish fleet — which itself was sunk during a great cyclone which hit the Azores a few days later. In 1596 Drake and Hawkins died during an unsuccessful attack on Spanish colonies in the West Indies.

Meanwhile Spain had captured Calais from France. In 1596 an English expedition against Calais was led by Howard of Effingham; the land forces were led by Elizabeth's young favourite, Essex, while Raleigh (*pic. 10*) was another of the courtier-soldiers who took part in the attack. The expedition took two ships, burnt two more, and forced the Spaniards to set fire to 50 others, to prevent their treasure being captured by the hated English. Essex also stormed the town and did the same to two others as he made his way home.

In 1596 a second great Armada was caught in a storm as it left Spanish waters — and some thirty ships were lost. In 1597 Essex and Raleigh failed to destroy a third Armada which managed to sail as far as the Channel before, once more, storms drove back most of the vessels.

In 1598 Philip of Spain died. The new rulers of Spain, like the rulers of France, were anxious to make a general peace. In England the cautious Burghley had died just before Philip of Spain; his son Robert was less influential than his father had been. The aging Queen took the advice of the dashing Essex who persuaded her to continue to make war on Spain, which was aiding the Irish rebels (Chapter 10). In 1600 a fourth Armada sailed but again failed to reach England. In 1601 a force of 4,000 Spaniards managed to land at Kinsale in Southern Ireland, but they were quickly besieged and could not save the Irish from defeat.

So Elizabeth's sailors defeated Spain at sea, while her forces in Ireland put down Spanish-inspired rebellions in that country. The last years of the Queen's reign also saw the success of English regiments in Dutch pay. They helped to defeat the Spaniards in the battles of Turnhout and Nieuport (*pic. 49*), the first defeats of Spanish forces in open land-battle. Prince Maurice of Nassau, son of William the Silent, made the Dutch army the finest in Europe. In doing so, he also taught Englishmen how to fight and win on land. In the seventeenth century English soldiers were to use their newly acquired skills to make England even greater than it had been under Elizabeth.

THE YOUNG HISTORIAN

1 Write extracts from a diary which might have been kept by a long-serving soldier about (i) an attack on a town (*pic. 45*) (he might have written about his pike, his uniform, the town walls, the problems of getting enough food, the deaths of friends and the capture of the town); (ii) events in 1585-86 under Leicester's command; (iii) events in 1597 under Essex; (iv) his employment by the Dutch in 1598-1600.

2 Write the letter which Elizabeth might have sent to Walsingham, explaining why she did not want a full-scale war in the Netherlands in the 1570s.

3 Draw or paint (i) a Spanish galleon (*pic. 46*); (ii) an English warship (*pic. 47*); and "The Armada Elizabeth" (*pic. 50*).

4 Make the posters which might have been used by (i) Hawkins inviting recruits to his enlarged Navy; (ii) men of Plymouth celebrating the defeat of the Armada; and (iii) Dutch Protestants looking for English recruits to their armies after 1598.

5 Write the headlines which might have appeared above reports on (i) the expulsion of the "sea-beggars" from Dover — in French, Spanish, English and Dutch Protestant papers; (ii) the Massacre of San Juan de Ulua — in newspapers in Madrid and Plymouth; (iii) Drake's arrival home after his attack in 1572 — in newspapers in Madrid and Plymouth; (iv) the Spanish capture of Antwerp — in newspapers owned by Spaniards, Frenchmen, Englishmen and Dutch Protestants; (v) Hawkins's appointment in 1577; (vi) the attack on Cadiz — in newspapers in London and Madrid; (vii) the defeat of the Armada — in newspapers in London, Paris and Madrid; (viii) the attack on Calais, 1596 — in newspapers in London, Paris and Madrid.

6 Make an illustrated time-chart to show the changing relationship between England, Spain, France and the Netherlands between 1558 and 1603. Write a brief note to explain the main changes in Elizabeth's policies.

7 Write the obituaries (or death notices) which might have appeared after the death of Hawkins or Drake (*pic. 48*).

10 Elizabethan England and the rest of the British Isles

The English Tudors and the Scottish Stuarts

In the thirteenth and fourteenth centuries English Kings had tried — and failed — to conquer Scotland. The names of Scotland's heroes — Wallace, Bruce and others — as well as the names of great battles, such as Bannockburn, are part of Scottish legend and folklore. And while England struggled to subdue Scotland, France took advantage of England's difficulties. For France was anxious to win back for herself the territories which English Kings claimed in France itself. So, traditionally, Scotland and France were allies against England.

Henry VII, the first of the Tudor Kings, knew that his hold on the throne was a very precarious one. By a number of policies, he tried to strengthen that uncertain hold. One of these involved a marriage between James IV of Scotland and Henry's daughter, Margaret Tudor. But even this marriage did not lead to peace or unity between England and Scotland. Henry VIII and the Protector Somerset led armies against Scotland. King James IV and "the flower of the Scottish nobility" were killed at the Battle of Flodden in 1513. In 1542 James V died, a few days after the Scots suffered a crushing defeat at Solway Moss.

51 Mary of Guise, the French mother of Mary, Queen of Scots and Catholic Regent of Scotland during her daughter's childhood.

52 John Knox, the powerful ▶ preacher and leader of the Scottish Reformation preaching to the Court in Scotland.

Mary of Guise (pic. 51)

The death of James V left his one-week old daughter, Mary, as Queen of Scots (*pic. 28*). Her mother, a French princess, Mary of Guise, lived in Scotland acting as Queen-Mother, or Regent, on her baby daughter's behalf.

We have seen that the young Princess was betrothed to the Dauphin of France, heir to the French throne. Mary, Queen of Scots, was sent to live in France while her mother ruled in Scotland. During those years (1542-60) the influence of the Reformation began to be felt in Scotland. A Protestant party grew up to support the extremist views of the Reformers who wanted to allow each local congregation to run its own church. These Presbyterians were opposed to the rule of the French Regent and to the Catholicism which was the official religion of her Court.

John Knox

Many Scottish reformers had been forced at some point to leave their own country. Some went to live in Geneva where they came under the influence of John Calvin, the extremist reformer. When Mary of Guise showed that she did not intend to persecute the Protestants, some of these exiles returned. John Knox (*pic. 52*) was a noted preacher who won a great following among the Presbyterians. He preached against there being bishops; he also demanded that services should be simple — no Mass, no vestments, no candles and little music. He wanted churches to be plain meeting-places — without stained-glass windows, statues, decorated altars and the like. Roused by the fire of Knox's preaching, the Scottish Protestants attacked and sacked many churches,

smashing the statues and stained-glass windows. The Regent got troops in from France to try to restore order. But this angered the Scots; the Protestants declared her deposed.

However, at that very time (1559) Mary, Queen of Scots, became Queen of France as her husband became King. It seemed certain that she would persuade him to send troops to restore order and Catholicism in Scotland. That raised the problem for the Scottish Protestants. Would they be able to stand up to a French attack? It was also a problem for Elizabeth. Should she go to the help of the Scottish Protestants or stand aside and watch French influence expand into Scotland?

A War, 1559-60

Elizabeth was anxious not to go to war. She did not approve of rebels in principle — fearing that their success might encourage someone to lead a similar rebellion against her in England. Nor did she approve of the extremist policies of Knox and the Protestants. Finally, she did not want to spend money on war — for fear that this might force her to ask for a meeting of Parliament.

But Walsingham (*pic. 17*) and other extremist Protestants persuaded her that she could not allow the Franco-Scottish alliance to go unchallenged — particularly when Mary, Queen of Scots, might prove to be a Catholic challenger to Elizabeth's own throne. And so money, supplies, ships and soldiers (*pic. 45*) were sent to help the Protestant rebels.

In 1560 they forced Mary of Guise to sign the Treaty of Edinburgh. This stated that the Scots recognized Elizabeth I as Queen of England. It also said that the French armies would withdraw from Scotland, and so the Protestants, under Knox, had the go-ahead for a sweeping Reformation. They announced that the Pope was no longer recognized in Scotland, that Catholic services had to end, and that the Presbyterian system was to be the Scottish way.

Mary, Queen of Scots

We have seen that in 1561 Mary Stuart returned to rule over her native land after the death of her French husband-King. (Her mother, Mary of Guise, had died by this time.) She did not try to undo the work of Knox and the Protestants, although she remained a faithful Catholic who hoped to win her country back to the true faith. Her private secretary, David Rizzio, had a great influence over her, particularly when her husband, Darnley (*pic. 31*), showed that he was unfit to be her husband. Darnley conspired with the Protestant Lords to get rid of Rizzio (*pic. 53*), so that there would be less danger of Catholicism being restored.

We have seen something of the unhappy history of Mary after that murder (Chapter 6). After her execution in 1587 (*pic. 33*), Mary's (and Darnley's) son became King James VI of Scotland. He was careful to avoid renewing

53 The murder of David Rizzio by Darnley's friends, the Protestant lords.

the French alliance and did not make war on Elizabeth. He had protested against his mother's execution — but not too strongly — and certainly he had not tried to seek revenge; he opposed Knox and his Presbyterian successors, but did not become a Catholic himself.

A Stuart King
During the last three years of Elizabeth's life there was great concern over the succession to the throne. Robert Cecil wanted Elizabeth to announce that James VI of Scotland should succeed her. But she made no such declaration. However, Cecil made sure that arrangements were made to put the Scottish Stuart on the throne. In 1603 the sixty-nine-year-old Queen was taken fatally ill. A few hours after she died, Cecil called a meeting of the Privy Council which confirmed the proclamation of James as James I of England — so the two countries came under the same ruler.

54   Carlow town in Ireland with its Norman castle dominating the bridge and weir.

Norman Ireland

From as early as Henry II's reign in the 12th century the English had claimed the right to rule Ireland. Norman barons were given land-holdings on which they built the formidable castles which dominated the countryside (*pic. 54*). These Norman lords were in constant conflict with the native Irish who were naturally opposed to the setting up of an English system of government in their country.

Elizabethan expansion

At first, the majority of Normans had lived in or around Dublin — inside the Pale, as it was called. But during Elizabeth's reign there was an attempt to bring the whole of Ireland under English rule. Slowly, English armies marched out of the Pale, conquering Leinster and Munster. In the north, in Ulster, they relied on an alliance with the most important Ulster chieftain, Hugh O'Neill, who was made the Earl of Tyrone by a grateful government.

But in 1595 Tyrone decided that he would try to form a united Catholic Ireland under his rule. He asked for Spanish help and appealed to Irishmen in Leinster, Munster and Connaught to rally around his flag. In 1596 Philip of Spain sent off a second Armada to try to get help to Tyrone. But, as we have seen, that Armada was wrecked by storms as soon as it left Spanish waters. Tyrone had to struggle on against English power.

Essex and Ireland

Essex had played a part in attacks on Spanish territory in 1596 and 1597. After the cautious Burghley had died in 1598, and the aging Queen had come under the influence of the dashing, ambitious Essex, he asked in 1599 for permission and authority to crush Tyrone's rebellion. He was appointed Governor General of Ireland, and given great supplies of money and troops with which he went off to conquer the country (*pic. 55*).

He issued a series of laws for his armies and set about to defeat the Irish. But he found that it was impossible to defeat this enemy — who did not stand and fight but, having attacked, ran into the wild and trackless countryside where Essex's soldiers were unable to catch them. Essex lost thousands of men in useless engagements with small groups of Irish guerillas. He became dispirited and asked Tyrone for a truce.

We have seen that this, together with his reckless behaviour, led to Essex's downfall and death in 1601. Meanwhile, in 1600, a fourth Armada sailed, but did not reach Ireland. In 1601 a force of 4,000 Spaniards landed at Kinsale in

55 Essex as Governor General of the Kingdom of Ireland — for other titles see the panel, top right. Notice the ships — a reminder of Essex's exploits with Howard of Effingham and Raleigh — and the armies on the march.

HIC TVVS ILLE COMES GENEROSA ESSEXIA NOSTRIS
QVEM QVAM GAVDEMVS REBVS ADESSE DVCEM.

the south of Ireland. They were quickly besieged and forced to surrender. The Irish rebels found that the new English commander, Lord Mountjoy, was more determined than Essex. Slowly but surely he defeated the rebels in Munster. Then he marched to attack Tyrone in Ulster. By 1603, as the Queen lay dying, Tyrone was on the point of surrender. The dying Queen had the pleasure of knowing that her forces were now in almost complete control of Ireland.

THE YOUNG HISTORIAN

1 Make a table of succession, showing how James VI of Scotland became James I of England (*pic. 28*). You might illustrate your table with ornamental writing or with small decorated portraits as seen in *pic. 1*.
2 Write the letters which might have been sent by Mary of Guise (*pic. 51*) and John Knox (*pic. 52*), concerning the other's policies.
3 Make the headlines which might have appeared above reports of (i) the return of Knox from Geneva; (ii) attacks on Catholic property — in newspapers supporting (a) Knox, (b) the Catholic Church in Scotland.
4 Write extracts from a diary which Elizabeth I might have kept and in which she wrote about her policy towards Scotland in 1559-60. (She might have wondered whether she ought to help the Protestants or not; and noted why she finally decided to send help and what was the result of her policy. She might also have written about Mary, Queen of Scots — *pic. 29.*)
5 Write the headlines which might have appeared above reports of the accession of James I, in newspapers owned by (i) Catholics and (ii) Puritans in England, and by (iii) Scotsmen.
6 Explain why English armies were unable to defeat the Irish Catholics in the 1590s.
7 Make a collage of possible headlines about Essex's (i) appointment to Ireland, (ii) truce with Tyrone, (iii) return to England and (iv) execution — imagining how they might have appeared in newspapers owned by (a) Tyrone, (b) Essex's friends and (c) a friend of Robert Cecil.
8 Write the letter which Tyrone might have sent asking for Philip's help against England. Explain why no help came until 1601.

11 Expanding Foreign Trade

The woollen industry

For many centuries before Elizabeth I England's prosperity had depended on its famous wool trade. In Yorkshire and East Anglia, in the Chilterns and the West Country, English sheep farmers bred huge flocks which produced the wool for them to sell at the markets to merchants from other parts of England and from Flanders and Italy. The export of this wool was under the control of the Merchants of the Staple, a group formed by previous Kings, to collect the heavy taxes imposed on exported wool and generally to supervise the export. Until the 1550s all exported wool had to pass through Calais, where the Merchants of the Staple had their headquarters.

But English Kings had long realized that they would be more sensible to encourage English people to take up the spinning and weaving (*pic. 56*) of wool for themselves. England could then export the finished cloth rather than just the raw wool which was worth less. The cloth industry might have grown more slowly than it did, had it not been for the Protestant immigrants who came to England to escape from persecution in their own country. The Flemish Protestants, persecuted by Philip of Spain, were settled in Norwich and Colchester, Gloucester and Bristol and other towns in the Cotswolds, East Anglia, Somerset and Devon. They taught the English how to develop their own cloth industry.

Merchant Adventurers

The export of raw wool was the business of the Merchants of the Staple. The export of woollen cloth was in the hands of another group of merchants — the Merchant Adventurers. From 1450 their main base in Europe was Antwerp (*pic. 49*). The fact that they used this town in the Netherlands as their base was a sign that the main centres of trade had passed from the Mediterranean (particularly Genoa and Venice) to the Atlantic coast — particularly to England and Holland.

Other industries

Now that her main export was cloth and not raw wool, England was a manufacturing as well as an agricultural country. The Protestant refugees also taught the English other trades, such as silk-weaving and lace-making. And there were other industries too; coal was mined, for use as fuel in larger homes as well as in some industries — for example, the making of salt, sugar and soap. The

Elizabethan government also encouraged the development of the mining industry — copper, tin, zinc and lead were mined in increasing quantities. The smelting of iron (*pic. 57*), the making of cutlery, glass and paper, the casting of guns, the building of ships, these and other industries grew.

The difficulties of foreign trade

It is important to remember that the exporting of goods was a hazardous affair. There was the problem of carrying the goods in England itself. The poor quality of both the roads and the carts meant that goods were often damaged or destroyed in transit (*pic. 58*). And it was also dangerous to sail, even the short distance to Europe, in the small ships of the time (*pic. 47*). Once the goods arrived in Europe, there was, in Elizabethan times, an ever-increasing danger arising from the religious wars of the period and also from pirates.

The religious wars engulfed France and the Netherlands and led to a fall in the volume of trade. This drove English merchants to look for other markets for their goods.

Chartered Companies

Few, if any, merchants wanted to venture into the unknown world looking for new markets on their own. Even when trading with nearby Europe, cloth merchants had co-operated to form the Company of Merchant Adventurers, which allowed the individual merchant to trade on his own — but within rules that it laid down — and which offered him the assistance of the Company's officials when he got his goods to Europe. It is not surprising that, when

56 A window showing some of the processes involved in clothmaking. Bottom left, the slaughterer at work. Centre left, the cropper using his shears to remove the nap which has been raised on the cloth by a workman using a teasel (centre right). Top left, the fuller mixing the fuller's earth into the wool so that it became thickened. Top right, stretching the finished cloth on tenterhooks.

57 The ironmaster at work in his small workshop, where he had a furnace in which to smelt the iron with charcoal.

Elizabethan merchants began to trade in the wider world, they did so through co-operative ventures and formed a number of Companies. Each Company that was formed asked the Queen for a Charter — a royal approval for the rules by which they wanted to govern their trade. Hence the name given to these groups of merchants — Chartered Companies. The Charter would usually give the Company the monopoly of trade within a certain area — Russia, Turkey, India or wherever. This encouraged merchants to take part in the risky business of foreign trade. Some traded on their own, inside the rules of the Company. But there was also a new development, of the "joint stock venture" whereby a number of men put their money into the Company which bought the ships, paid the sailors and organized the trade. Profits were then shared out among the investors in proportion to each man's stake in the venture. The man who put in £100 only got half as much profit as the man who had put in £200.

Richard Chancellor

In 1555, while Mary was still on the throne, the Merchant Adventurers fitted out three ships which were intended to sail westwards, in search of a route to the Spice Islands off the East Indies. The ships became separated off New-foundland (*pic. 59*). Two of them, commanded by Sir Hugh Willoughby, took refuge in a harbour in Lapland and unfortunately the crews died during

58 A horse-drawn litter. These were safer than waggons which were likely to tip over. But merchants had to use such primitive carts on the poor-quality roads and tracks.

the Arctic winter. The third ship, commanded by Richard Chancellor, sailed round the North Cape, found the entrance to the White Sea and came to the fishing village of Archangel in northern Russia.

Chancellor then followed the old Viking routes into Russia — along great rivers — and made his way to Moscow where he met the Tsar, Ivan the Terrible. The Tsar gave Chancellor many trading privileges and in 1556 sent the first Russian ambassador to London (*pic. 13*).

The Muscovy Company

The merchants who had paid for the expedition by Willoughby and Chancellor now formed another company for the purpose of developing the trading privileges granted by the Tsar. They called themselves the Muscovy Company and they used the route to Archangel to send English cloth to Russia, where it soon became popular with the people in that cold climate. In return, the merchants brought back furs, timber and hemp which were in demand in England and which had previously been bought from German traders.

In 1557 the directors of the Muscovy Company chose Anthony Jenkinson to lead a fleet to Russia, where he was to set up trading stations from which later fleets could pick up goods. Jenkinson commanded four ships and took with him the Russian ambassador to London. Having completed the tasks given him by his directors, Jenkinson then looked further afield for trade. He made his way south until he came to the Caspian Sea (*pic. 60*). He then went on into Persia where he established new trading stations in 1559. Elizabeth's advisers were delighted with the success of this venture, which led to increased employment for cloth-makers and ship-builders, and for sailors, while also ensuring a regular supply of timber, furs and other goods which were wanted in England.

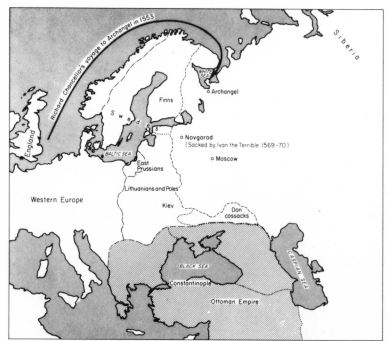

59 Chancellor's voyage, 1553.

60 Jenkinson's voyage, 1557-59. ►

The Levant Company

The success of the Muscovy Company encouraged other merchants to look for another route to the East Indies — which had been the original aim of the Chancellor voyage. Some merchants founded the Levant Company with the intention of developing English trade with the Turkish-held lands in the Eastern Mediterranean. The Turkish ruler gave the company the right to trade and to build trading posts or factories in Turkey, Asia Minor and Egypt.

Richard Hakluyt

Hakluyt was an Elizabethan who encouraged his countrymen to look for new lands — we shall examine the work of some Elizabethan explorers in Chapter 12. He also wrote about the work of those who followed his advice — the rich merchants and landowners (*pic. 61*) who provided the money for the fleets which sailed to the distant parts of the world.

Writing in 1589 he noted:

At that time our merchants perceived the commodities and wares of England to be in small request with the countries and people about us, and near unto us, and that those merchandises which strangers, in the time and memory of our ancestors, did earnestly seek and desire, were now neglected and the price thereof abated, although by us carried to their own ports, and all foreign merchandisers in great account and their prices wonderfully raised, certain grave citizens of London, and men of great wisdom, and careful of the good of their country, began to think with themselves how this mischief might be remedied . . . for seeing that the wealth of the Spaniards and the Portuguese, by the discovery and search of new trades and countries,

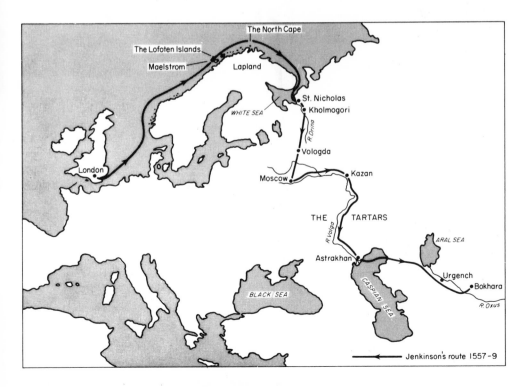

81

was marvellously increased, supposing the same to be a course and means for them also to obtain the like, they thereupon resolved upon a new and strange navigation.

Increased trade, it was thought, would lead to increased employment and so to a decline in the number of beggars (*pic. 62*).

To India

Between 1585 and 1591 John Newbery and Ralph Fitch set out on a series of journeys and finally arrived in India. They travelled overland from Syria, sailed down the Persian Gulf to Hormuz, then crossed to Goa and so to the then capital of India, Agra, where Fitch met the Emperor, or Mogul, Akbar. Newbery had died on the way, but Fitch went on down the Ganges, through the Bay of Bengal to Burma, Siam, Malacca and then made his way home via Ceylon, Hormuz, Baghdad and Aleppo.

When Fitch got home in 1591, England had defeated the Armada, and Drake had sailed around the world. In that year, too, Lancaster sailed around the Cape of Good Hope and made his way to India. Englishmen were at last able

61 A miniature of an English gentleman by Nicholas Hilliard (1547-1619). It was gentlemen such as this who commanded the ships which sailed the world, who financed and organized the Companies which enlarged English trade in the Elizabethan period, and who fought the Spaniards in the Netherlands and Ireland.

82

to do what the Spanish and Portuguese — but no one else — had been doing for a century.

Other voyages to India encouraged some merchants of the Levant Company to form a new Company for the opening of trade with the East. On 31 December 1600 they were granted a Charter which established the East India Company. Its first expeditions were not a great success. But the following letter of 1614 from Jehangir Khan, the ruler of India, shows that by then English traders were well received in India.

The letter of love and friendship which you sent, and the presents, tokens of your good affection towards me, I have received by the hands of your ambassador, Sir Thomas Roe (who well deserveth to be your trusted servant), upon which mine eyes were so fixed that I could not easily remove them to any other object . . . .

Upon which assurance of your royal love I have given my general command to all the kingdoms and ports of my dominions to receive all the merchants of the English nation as the subjects of my friend; that in what place soever they choose to live, they may have reception and residence to their own content and safety; and what goods soever they desire to sell or buy, they may have free liberty; and at what port soever they shall arrive, neither Portugal nor any other shall dare to molest their quiet . . . . (They shall be free) to sell, buy, and to transport into their country at their pleasure.

The outline of the future development of English trading was now clear, and it was this trade which provided the money and the spur to the industrial development which in the 18th century made Britain the strongest power in the world. The seeds of that strength had been sown by Elizabethan merchants and venturers.

62 There was a great increase in the number of the poor during the Elizabethan period, as they had lost the refuge they had once relied on from the monasteries, and because the new sheep-farming needed fewer people than had been employed in the past on arable farms. Elizabethan laws compelled each parish to look after its own poor. Elizabeth's merchants helped to provide more work for people when they developed new markets for English goods.

THE YOUNG HISTORIAN

1 Write the letter which might have been sent by a merchant, explaining the reasons for forming the Company of Merchant Adventurers and the development of the cloth trade.

2 Using Hakluyt's article as the basis for your answer, explain why there was a need to develop new markets for Elizabethan trade. (*Pic. 62* will also be useful.)

3 Write the article which might have appeared in 1603 in which an Elizabethan compares the extent of foreign trade in 1603 with that in 1558. (He might have written about various voyages, new Companies, new countries, the financing of Companies and the growth of confidence during the last twenty years of Elizabeth's reign.)

4 Write the headlines which might have appeared above newspaper reports of (i) the arrival of Protestant immigrants in Norwich; (ii) the formation of the Muscovy Company.

5 Write an account of the formation of a Chartered Company to show why and how it came into existence. (You might want to use *pic. 61* as the basis for a piece on the rich Elizabethan who had money to invest; *pic. 56* for something on the growth of the cloth industry; *pics. 59 and 60* for something about the development of trade with new countries; and *pics. 13, 40 and 50* to remind you of how the merchants in the Company would ask the Queen for a Charter and a monopoly of trade.)

6 Write extracts from the diary which might have been kept by one of the following: (i) a merchant who was aware of the difficulties of foreign trade, (ii) someone who sailed with Chancellor (*pic. 59*), (iii) Jenkinson (*pic. 60*), (iv) Ralph Fitch.

7 Paint or draw your own version of *either* English merchants at the Tsar's Court *or* Chancellor's ship arriving at Archangel.

8 Make the posters which might have been used by (i) the Merchants of the Staple, warning merchants that they had to send their wool via Calais or (ii) the Levant Company, inviting people to buy a share in the Company.

12 The Elizabethan Foundations of Empire

New routes and the explorers

In 1453 the Turks captured Constantinople (now called Istanbul and in present-day Turkey) and closed the trade routes to China and India. While these routes had been open, the Mediterranean had been the centre of world trade. Venice and Genoa had been major international centres from which Marco Polo and others had sailed, and where Columbus and other famous explorers had had their first experience of the sea.

With the closing of the old routes, Portuguese and Spanish sailors set out to discover new routes to the East. Some followed the example of Vasco da Gama and sailed around the Cape of Good Hope and took the easterly direction; others followed the example of Magellan and sailed around the tip of South America to sail westwards to China and India.

Columbus, as you may know, sailed in that westerly direction in the hope of finding a route to India. But, as he and others discovered, the Continent of America was in the way (*pic. 63*).

63 A late sixteenth-century map showing that the Americas blocked the western route to the fabled wealth of China and the valuable spices of the Moluccas.

The Papal division of the world

In 1494 the Pope had recognized the growing power of Spain and Portugal by dividing the area of the world to be discovered between these two countries. He drew a line about 500 kilometres (350 miles) to the west of the Azores. Spain was given the right to explore and conquer all the lands to the west of that line, while Portugal had the same right over all land to the east of it.

Englishmen and the unknown world

During the reign of Henry VII (Elizabeth's grandfather) John Cabot was given the royal permission to sail in search of a new route to India. He imitated Columbus, sailed in a westerly direction and managed to reach Hudson's Bay in northern Canada — which he thought would provide a route to India. However, his men forced him to turn back because of the fierce cold and the danger from icebergs.

Henry VIII devoted his attention to trying to win back that French Empire which had been almost lost during the Hundred Years War — and Englishmen did not go exploring again until the 1550s.

The search for a North East passage

We have seen that Willoughby and Chancellor went off to look for another route to India via the North East (*pic. 59*). It is worth noting that their voyage was financed by the Merchant Adventurers under the governorship (or headship) of Sebastian Cabot, son of John Cabot. We have also seen that their journey led to increased trade with Russia (*pic. 60*) and Persia.

Back to the North West passage

But Chancellor, Jenkinson and others proved that there was no sea route via the North East to India, and so Englishmen decided to turn back to follow Cabot's path and, they hoped, to improve on his work. They knew the fortune that could be made by anyone who managed to make a successful voyage to and from the Spice Islands where spices could be bought cheaply (at about £1.75p for 50 kilos) and then sold expensively in Europe (at about £175

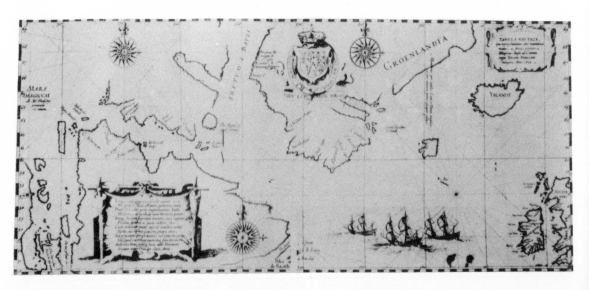

for 50 kilos). Even the small ships of this period could carry back tons of this valuable cargo and thus enrich the adventurers.

Martin Frobisher

In 1576 Martin Frobisher set sail with two ships, one of 20 tons and the other of 25 tons. His journey took him much further north than Cabot had gone. Just after he had passed Greenland, one of his ships had to return; Frobisher reached latitude 63° North, where he entered what he thought were the straits of Asia. He returned to England with some black mineral which proved to contain gold. This led to the formation of a Cathay (or China) Company. Courtiers (*pics. 40 and 61*) and merchants rushed to invest in this new enterprise.

Frobisher set off on a second voyage in 1577, taking with him three ships for the purpose of bringing back gold. But very little gold was extracted from the three shiploads of rock which he brought back.

He set off on a third voyage in 1578, mainly to found a colony on what we now call Baffin Island, off the coast of Canada. 40 sailors, 30 miners and 30 soldiers went with him to explore their new colony, to make further search for the passage to India, and to prepare great quantities of ore for shipping back to England. But when they reached Frobisher Bay they found it frozen over, so that they could not make their way through to the East. The ship carrying materials for building houses was sunk, and they sailed in storm and fog until they reached what we now call the Hudson Strait. Finally they did reach Frobisher Strait where they collected their ore — but, instead of starting a colony, returned home. This ore, too, proved almost valueless. The Cathay Company went bankrupt because it could not get back the money it had spent on the three voyages.

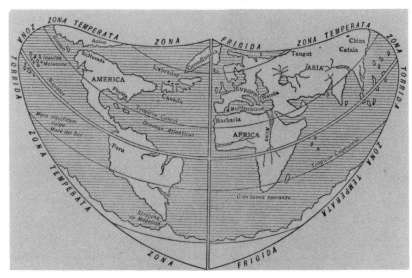

◄ 64 A chart made by Henry Hudson after his second voyage, showing the approaches to what we now call Hudson's Bay.

65 Sir Humphrey Gilbert's own map of the world — showing that mythical passage to the North West.

Frobisher did not make any more voyages to the North West. He commanded a ship in the battle against the Armada and died fighting against the Spanish in Brittany. Forty years later Frobisher's example was followed by Henry Hudson (*pic 64*), and although his work, too, seemed to have failed, his name is commemorated in the great Hudson's Bay Company formed in 1670 to control English trade with the country which we now call Canada — and which became part of the British Empire in 1763.

Sir Humphrey Gilbert

Most English seamen seemed to concentrate at this time on one of three things. Some were content to trade with the Spanish and Portuguese colonies. Others wanted to set up new trading posts in Russia, the Levant and India (Chapter 11). A large number seemed to be concerned only with annoying the Spaniards whose ships were attacked and whose colonies they tried to plunder.

Sir Humphrey Gilbert may not have been as famous as Hawkins, Drake (*pic. 48*) or Raleigh (*pic. 10*). But his work was much more important than theirs and it is a pity that more of the sea-dogs did not imitate him.

Gilbert was Member of Parliament for Plymouth, a stepbrother of Raleigh's and he wanted Elizabeth to challenge Spain by founding colonies in undeveloped parts of the world. In 1577 he wrote:

And the diminishing of their forces . . . is to be done either by open hostility or by some colourable means; as by giving licence . . . to discover and inhabit some strange place . . . .

The way to work the feat is to set forth . . . certain ships of war to the New Land, which, with your good licence, I will undertake without your Majesty's expense . . . . The setting forth of shipping for this service will amount to no great matter, and the return shall certainly be with great gain. For the Newland fish is a rich . . . merchandise. And by the gain thereof, shipping, victual, munition and the transporting of five or six thousand soldiers may be defrayed . . . . If your Highness will permit me with my

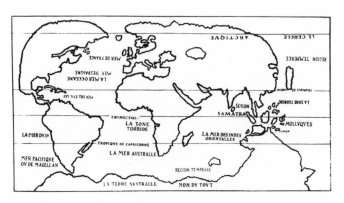

66 This world map drawn in 1546 shows that men had some knowledge of Australia.

associates . . . to perform the aforesaid enterprise, then . . . such a competent company [may be] transported to the West Indies as may be able not only to dispossess the Spaniards thereof, but also to possess forever your Majesty and realm therewith . . .

The first attempt to found a colony

In 1578 he persuaded the Queen to grant him a licence to set up colonies along the sea board of North America (*pic. 65*). This was meant to anger the Spaniards to whom, according to the Pope's ruling, this region belonged. In 1583 Gilbert took possession of St John's in Newfoundland and "signified unto all men that from that time forward they should take the same land as a territory belonging to the Queen of England and himself authorized under Her Majesty to enjoy it".

The colonists brought with them all they needed to start a new life — building-materials, tools and seeds for the farmers, animals and "music in good variety, toys and hobby horses . . . ". Having set up this first colony, Gilbert sailed to make another settlement. But one of his ships sank, and the colonists in it drowned off Nova Scotia. Gilbert, with two ships left, turned for England. He was in a ship of only 10 tons. This sank in a fierce storm off the Azores. Gilbert was drowned. Lacking his leadership and inspiration, the colony also collapsed. Life in the New World was more difficult than people had realized.

Spain versus English traders

Until about 1568 Drake (*pic. 48*) like Hawkins was content to trade with the existing Spanish colonies. Then the Spanish government passed a law forbidding foreign ships to trade in Spanish ports. Hawkins refused to accept this and continued to take slaves from Africa to the Spanish colonies where the planters and merchants were more interested in profitable trade than in laws passed by Philip II in Spain.

In 1568 Hawkins had sold his cargo of 500 slaves and was leading his six ships back to England when he was caught in a storm . His ships put back into San Juan de Ulua (now Vera Cruz) where they were attacked by ships of the Spanish navy. Drake managed to escape and get back to England (Chapter 9). His resolve grew to make his country stronger and Spain weaker.

Drake around the world, 1577-80

In 1577 Elizabeth I gave Drake one of her own ships and a large sum of money to help him fit out others, for a journey on which he intended to plunder the Spanish colonies in the Pacific — where they would not be expecting an attack. He commanded the *Pelican*, which he re-named the *Golden Hind*, and he had four other ships in his small fleet, which set out to sail through the Magellan Straits into the Pacific (*pic. 66*). He also hoped to find that southern continent of which there was some knowledge and which lay to the south of the Magellan Straits — what we now call Australasia.

The Spaniards were taken by surprise. Off the coast of Peru Drake captured the gold-carrying *Cacafuego*, and so made sure that his voyage would be profitable. He plundered cities such as Lima and Valparaiso, although by the time he sailed into the Pacific he was on his own as the other ships had either been sunk, or had returned home. Later he would command much larger fleets (*pic. 67*). But as he sailed across the Pacific in the *Golden Hind*, calling in at the Moluccas, he proved that English sailors could do what had previously been done only by the Spanish and Portuguese. He had opened a new route to the East, given greater confidence to the Elizabethans, and won for himself not only great wealth but also a title. For when the *Golden Hind* docked in Deptford in London in 1580, the Queen went aboard and knighted him as Sir Francis Drake.

Sir Walter Raleigh

Raleigh (*pic. 10*) was stepbrother to Gilbert. Born in Devon in 1552, he grew up in a period when Englishmen were achieving the self-confidence which came from increased wealth and power. In his own *Historie of the World* he wrote: "If therefore it be asked whether the Macedonian or the Roman were

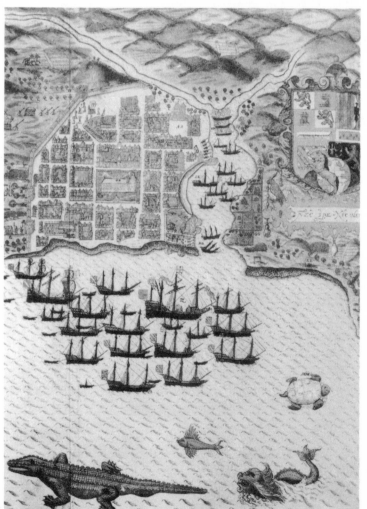

67   Drake in the West Indies.

68   A drawing made by John ➤ White of the first English settlement at Roanoke.

the best warrior, I will answer, 'The Englishman'." Elizabeth I had been attracted by this tall, handsome author-sailor. She had given him land in Ireland, and on Gilbert's death, permission to found colonies in America.

In 1584 his first expedition was more one of exploration than of colonization. His "fleet" consisted of two ships which reached the West Indies in June 1584 after a voyage lasting about seven weeks. In July they reached Florida and sailed until they found a safe harbour, further north, in what we now call North Carolina.

In 1585 Raleigh sent out a second expedition to the territory which he had named Virginia, in honour of the unmarried Queen. This expedition was led by Sir Richard Grenville, Raleigh's cousin. He took some colonists with him — and all the building-materials, animals, tools and so on that they would need to start a new life. Grenville settled the colonists at Roanoke (*pic. 68*).

Difficulties and failures

Among those who sailed on that second expedition was an artist, John White. His drawings (*pics. 68 and 69*) and the glowing reports of the commander on his return persuaded people that there was a glittering future for colonies in America. Hakluyt wrote enthusiastically about them; playwrights such as Ben

Jonson had their characters speak of "all the treasure . . . at their feete . . . gold more plentiful than copper is with us . . . rubies and diamonds gathered along the seashore . . .".

In fact, life was very hard. The colonists fought with the Indians, forgot to grow crops, became very short of food, and were glad to see Drake when he called in on his way home from the West Indies (*pic. 67*) in 1586. They persuaded Drake to take them home. When Grenville arrived with a relief expedition, he was annoyed to find the colony deserted.

In 1587 Raleigh sent out another group of colonists under the leadership of the artist, John White. Soon after their arrival White realized that they did not have the right supplies. He returned to England to organize a relief expedition. Unfortunately, he was prevented from doing so because of the Spanish War and the Armada. White did not return to Roanoke until 1590. All 150 colonists had disappeared. There were no signs of a massacre and it seems that the colonists had gone away of their own accord and died inland.

Raleigh out of favour

In 1595 Raleigh lost the Queen's favour by persuading one of her ladies-in-waiting to marry him. He was sent from Court. He tried to win back the jealous Queen's favour by organizing an expedition to Guiana on the northern coast of South America. Here he hoped to discover the empire which was believed to be ruled by the Golden King, El Dorado. He failed to find this legendary empire and returned home to fight, under Essex, against Spain. He took part

92

69 White's drawing of Indians fishing off the coast of Roanoke.

in the raid on Cadiz in 1596. On their return home he and Essex quarrelled. Raleigh may have been involved in the Essex plot of 1601. If so, he was fortunate to escape death.

On Elizabeth's death Raleigh was involved in a plot to get James I off the throne and to replace him with his cousin, Lady Arabella Stuart. He was imprisoned in the Tower (*pic. 20*) for twelve years. James released him so that he might undertake another expedition to El Dorado. When this led to a fight with the Spaniards, James I had Raleigh executed in 1618. The English still did not have a colony in the Americas. But Gilbert, Drake and Raleigh had shown the way. In the 17th century there would be colonies set up all along the eastern seaboard of North America — another sign of the growth of British power which had its roots in Elizabethan England.

THE YOUNG HISTORIAN

1 Explain why Columbus and Davis sailed westwards in search of the Indies. (You might want to mention spices, the Turks, the belief that there was a passage.)
2 Write the headlines which might have appeared in London newspapers about (i) the formation of the Cathay Company in 1576 and (ii) its bankruptcy in 1579.
3 Write an eyewitness account of the loading of the ships setting out on an expedition.
4 Write the letter which might have been sent by a rich courtier (*pics. 40 and 61*) explaining why he was investing his money in the expeditions looking for a North East passage (*pic. 64*). (He might have mentioned his hatred for Spain, and his wish to please Elizabeth I by helping to make England richer. See also the suggestions in question 1.)
5 Give an account of the difficulties facing Gilbert's colonists in 1583. You might write your answer as a long article from a newspaper, as a letter from a colonist, or as a series of extracts from a diary — which you might illustrate.
6 Write the headlines which might have appeared above reports on Drake when (i) he set sail in 1577, (ii) he sent back reports of the loss of some ships, (iii) news came of his attack on Spanish colonies in the Pacific, and (iv) he returned to London in 1580.
7 Write the letters which colonists in Roanoke might have sent in (i) 1585, (ii) 1586, (iii) 1587, and (iv) 1588 after White had left for England.
8 Write the obituaries (or death notices) which might have appeared about Gilbert, Drake or Raleigh.
9 Paint or draw your own version of one of the following: (i) founding a colony, (ii) attacking Spanish shipping, (iii) Elizabeth I knighting Sir Francis Drake.

Other Visual Aids

16 mm Films

Elizabethan England	Gateway
English Literature of the Elizabethan Period	Gateway
William Shakespeare	Rank
Sir Francis Drake	Rank
Elizabethan Houses and People	Gateway
The Age of Exploration: Part 3, The English and Dutch Explorers	Rank
Tudor Houses	Gateway

35 mm Filmstrips

Mary I	Common Ground
Elizabeth I	Common Ground
Reformation and Counter-Reformation	Visual Publications
Queen Elizabeth I and Her Times	Visual Information Services
Life in Elizabethan England	Common Ground
North East Passage	Visual Publications
North West Passage	Visual Publications
Sir Walter Raleigh	Visual Publications

Index

The numbers in **bold type** refer to pages on which illustrations appear